SPORTS TRADING
ON BETFAIR

**Profitable betting exchange
systems and strategies for
trading on Betfair and Betdaq**

WAYNE
BAILEY

CONTENTS

ACKNOWLEDGEMENTS

FIRST and foremost, I'd like to thank my late father, Archie Bailey, who introduced me to betting at an early age. People often frown upon the betting industry but some of the most amazing times in my life involved racecourses, risk, bookmakers and betting. It's a wonderful world to be involved in provided you don't take it to excess. My father was never a big gambler but from an early age, he taught me the importance of paying my debts and not being afraid to admit when I called it wrong. It's a lesson that has served me extremely well in other areas of life too. He came from a modest background but he had all sorts of ingenious ways of making money down through the years for his family, the likes of which would have left Del Boy in the shade. He was a great friend and is dearly missed every single day. Thanks too to my mother Bridget and my brother Alan who are always on hand to lend advice on any topic, through good times and bad. To my daughter Aislinn; you are a constant joy and remind me every day that there is more to life than work. Last but certainly not least, my long-suffering wife Krista deserves huge recognition for putting up with me. I've spent some time as a professional gambler and the ups and downs (in both money and mood) must be very difficult for any partner to deal with; yet she never complains and always lets me do my own thing. She's had to get on with family life while I tapped away on my laptop trading, punting and writing — and for that, I'm eternally grateful. This time next year love...

PREFACE

Saturday, 23rd June 2007 — Golden Jubilee Stakes (Ascot)
AS I sit motionless in my home office on my fancy swivel chair, the awful reality begins to sink in. I'm surprisingly calm. I've just lost a small fortune in the space of five minutes but I'm not even shouting, screaming or swearing. I just feel numb. I continue staring at the red figure in front of my eyes. It feels like a dream; a bad one at that. At the top of the screen, my Betfair account balance still reads £5,542.27 but I know that once I hit the refresh button, that figure would be reduced by around 90%. How can five grand disappear into thin air with a few clicks of a mouse? I accept that I was trading a little recklessly but I don't deserve this cruel fate. Perhaps sitting still and doing nothing is a good idea. I can put off the inevitable pain by doing nothing. Maybe there's been a mistake and Betfair will rectify it in a moment. Perhaps *Takeover Target* wasn't beaten by a head and the placings will be reversed. Maybe the commentator has called it wrong; my horse did hit 1.10 in-running after all, and looked like a cert. Surely there's been a mistake. The TV pictures are telling a different story though. I can't bear to watch the replay as I know it will show that *Soldier's Tale* won the race.

The 'Market Closed' message has just popped up on the screen and there's no way back.

I check my P&L (profit and loss) for the day hoping against hope that there's been some technical glitch and my bets weren't fired in. I know this is pure delusion though; after all, the matched bets were displayed right in front of my eyes just a moment ago. But I'm desperate for the reality I've created to go away and will clutch at any straws that are going. It's time to man up and face the truth. I go to the P&L button....

Click.

Wayne Bailey 23-Jun-2007
Horse Racing: -£5012.35 Total P&L: -£5012.35

There it is in black and white. There's no getting away from it. I say it out loud: "I, Wayne Bailey, have just lost five grand". Not quite the stuff of rogue trader Nick Leeson, but it's five grand I didn't really have to waste. I try to find the positives. Are there any? OK, I still have over a monkey (£500) in my account and that's a lot of money in any man's language right? But no, it's no comfort; the money left in my account means nothing now, it's just a figure. I need the account to get back to five grand; nothing else will do. I open up another market. I know this is all wrong but I put what's left in the account on a horse I vaguely remembered as having ability. The price hovers around 20.0. Those odds suggest that the horse only has a five percent chance of winning but I don't need it to win, I just need it to run well for a while so I can get a good trade. I'm desperate. I tell myself that if I'm not in profit in thirty seconds, I'll get out. A few hundred, that's all I need from this market. I could then use that profit for another trade and build the bank back up again on the next race. Perhaps things aren't so bad?

"And they're off..."

The horse gets a great start. I'm quickly in the green. Profit is mounting. £100...£150...£200...£250... I tell myself I'll trade out once I get another hundred quid profit. But I'm like the metaphorical rabbit in the headlights and I can't pull the trigger. Maybe the horse will win and then I'll have missed out on a massive payout. If it wins, I'll get my five grand back plus loads more. He's still going well... he actually might do this. Screw it, it's all or nothing, I'll let the bet stand. I begin to make deals with the Almighty.

"Please God, let this one go in, I promise I'll never trade recklessly again. In fact, I'll donate a few hundred to charity if it wins. Just get me out of this mess."

My jockey comes off the bridle but some others sit still. We are still a mile out — this isn't good. The green figure on my trading screen turns red. OK, this is madness. I have the option of taking a further one hundred quid loss. I know I should take it, At least I'd still have four hundred left, which is better than nothing. But again, I just can't seem to pull the trigger. The price keeps moving away — how the hell did I get myself into this mess? It's all happening so fast. I need to get away.

My wife calls me to say she's made me a cup of tea. The race isn't over but I go down to the kitchen anyway. Tea sounds nice; temporary relief from this awful situation. Perhaps when I go back and check, the horse will have somehow recovered and won the race and I'll be back in the black. Deep down, I know it won't happen.

My three-year-old daughter bangs a toy drum and I block my ears playfully. She laughs heartily and does it again. I'm surprised at how calm I am. The world still turns.

"How's the trading going today love?"

"Ah, tricky enough. I'm not really in tune with the markets."

"You lose a few quid?"

"Yeah. I think I'll cut my losses and call it a day, I'm a bit tired. Mind if I go for a pint later?"

"No probs."

She's great like that. She doesn't interfere and lets me do what I do. The problem is, what I've been doing today has been all wrong.

I walk back to the computer room and close the door. I click the refresh button:

Account balance: £0.00

INTRODUCTION

YOU might be thinking that a story about losing five and-a-half grand is not the best way to kick off a book which gives advice about trading; but I'm guessing that certain readers will have been down a similar path before and will have some understanding of how even the most disciplined traders can end up throwing caution to the wind on occasion. Perhaps you lost more than five grand, perhaps it was far less — but blowing up a bank is something most of us have done, often more than once. I share the story because I want to offer some hope to people who are down that lonely road of losing money and acting stupidly. I want to tell them that it is possible to bounce back and eventually make steady profits from trading. I know because I've been there. It's hard, but it is possible. Having said that, this book is not intended to be some sort of 'get out' strategy for those with gambling addictions, or those who may be in financial trouble. This book makes no claims or guarantees and it certainly won't assist those who are in debt from gambling. Trading should only be carried out with money you can afford to lose and if you suspect you have a problem, you should seek help.

Getting back to the earlier story — I've included my clanger of a mistake as it highlights the type of situation that traders need to avoid at all costs. There may also be readers who have never been reckless with their trading (although I suspect those numbers are few and far between) and the story should make them think twice if they're ever tempted to let their discipline become lax.

On that occasion, I was having a losing day so I foolishly decided to take a gamble and trade inplay on *Takeover Target*; with dire consequences. I knew what I was doing was wrong but sometimes, the thoughts of having a losing day can seem too much to handle and overwhelmed with emotion and fear, we do crazy things. I've since learned to manage that overwhelming feeling and my account is much healthier for having done so. The funny thing is, I was initially down just thirty quid that day. But I just didn't want to accept a losing day. Instead of taking a thirty quid hit, I created a five grand loss. Madness.

Despite the fact that I'd spent other successful periods in my life as a professional gambler, I found the transition to trading difficult. Back then, I was making the classic mistakes; I'd pick up lots of small wins but then I'd wipe it all out with one huge loss. But for me, the changes I made to turn myself from a losing trader to a reasonably good one were not all that big. Discipline, correct staking and eliminating over-trading were some of the main things I worked on and the biggest lesson I've learned is that it pays to keep things simple. The thing that makes trading most difficult is our ego and the fear of being wrong — and this is especially true of the male sex, which make up the vast majority of the trading population. It really is true to say that we are our own worst enemy most of the time.

We all know that we have to accept losing trades along the way but this is actually a very difficult thing to do. The urge to have our opinion validated and get back in profit to prove to the world and ourselves that we are a savvy trader can be overwhelming. As I say, I had enjoyed success as a horse racing punter in the past and wanted to feel that success again in the trading environment. I can't think of any other profession which sees common sense get chucked out the window as often as it does in trading, and the results can be disastrous, as illustrated in the preface. That includes financial trading too of course. For an even more spectacular example, just look at the recent banking crises in the UK, Ireland, the US and many other countries around the world.

It's kind of funny when you think about it: trading (be it financial trading or sports trading) is a profession which will see well over 90% of its participants lose money. Yet there is no shortage of people queuing up to try it out. Some will lose so much money that they will go bankrupt. One financial trader friend of mine lost everything he had including his family, as they had simply had enough of his ways. It's often a sad and lonely business and has left many casualties strewn along the way. What other profession offers you a 90% chance that you won't get paid at the end of the year — with the possibility of bankruptcy thrown in as your bonus?

But for those that make it, the rewards can be great. And that's what makes trading so appealing. Yes, you can lose a fortune — but there's always the hope of winning one too.

Having won and lost fairly big sums through the years, I've come to realise that trading is around 70% psychological and 30% strategy. It took me a long time to learn that my own worst enemy was myself and I've since spent a lot of time working on the mental side of things, rather than looking for the next great set-up or system. I'm not a psychologist, but I've a deep interest in the workings of the human mind and in these pages I hope I can offer some insight and advice on how to stop your primitive brain from taking over your 21st Century one. Alongside some of the strategies I use myself, I hope the book proves informative, honest and somewhat entertaining.

When you bought this book, you weren't expecting a biography of Wayne Bailey and I don't want to bore people to tears telling them about my life. However, when I decided to write a book, I made my mind up that I would avoid the things that annoy me about other trading books, and something which often bugs me when I'm reading a book about trading is the lack of personality and passion from the author. So often, the author just churns out graphs and figures making the book hard work to read. Sometimes, I wonder if these authors are actually traders at all. I don't want to go down that formula route. Trading is exciting, dynamic and dangerous too. I've seen great highs and very low times and have made all the mistakes along the way that can be made. I hope to share some of this experience with the readers so forgive me if my writing style is not always formal, and because I usually trade on horseracing, most of the examples in this book are from that sport. However the same principles can be applied in other sports too so I hope the non-racing traders won't be too disappointed.

I don't declare to be an expert or any kind of authority on trading and I won't promise that this book will make you riches. From the outset, I want to make it clear that these strategies are not foolproof and there is no great system out there that will make you constant money. A few sentences ago, I mentioned that trading is a *dynamic* business; in other words it is constantly changing. Therefore, what works this year may not work next year. Markets and their participants adjust over time and no matter how good an edge you may have in one particular area, it won't last forever. The strategies and tactics outlined in this book are working for me now but it would be irresponsible for me to suggest that they will always do so in the future. That said, I've found that the best trading and betting books I've read are ones that give me new ideas to try, and sometimes I can adapt or adjust the author's strategies to suit my needs. Hopefully, you will get some ideas in these pages that spur you on and create a desire to try new things.

Trading is very hard and being frank, most people don't have the mentality for it. Therefore, the sad reality is that most people reading this book will probably lose money trading. Does this mean that this book has failed in its purpose? I don't think so. I just think it's best to be honest. People are tired of the 'get rich quick' lies and I hope that readers will appreciate this book for what it is: a genuine attempt to help people become better traders and understand the markets — with no promises attached. I know plenty of otherwise highly intelligent people that lose their head when they try to trade and no amount of coaching can change their personality. So I'd be lying if I said I could turn a reader that I've never met into a profitable trader. What I can offer, though, is a decade of experience including all the ups and downs those ten years of trading entailed. Simple as that. If you get some new ideas from the book, use some of mine, or even just increase your knowledge of how and why odds move, then the book will have done its job.

Early on in my trading career, I lost serious amounts of cash before I finally had a long hard look at myself and where my frivolous approach to money was leading to. What I'm trying to say is that I've been there, done that, worn the T-shirt, lost the T-shirt — and finally found it again. It took a few years before I started to churn a regular profit. For every reader that has felt despair, been depressed or exasperated from trading, I hope they find comfort that this author has been in that place too.

But it's not all doom and gloom. Trading has provided me with some incredible highs too and I've met many great people, both online and offline since I began. I've had some fantastic wins and trading has challenged my mind and made me open to new ideas and possibilities. It certainly keeps the brain ticking over, that's for sure. Clocking up a winning day, then week, then month feels fantastic and the sense of achievement can be incredible. And spending money that you've more or less created out of thin air is amazing too so I don't want to just focus on the negatives.

There'll never be a way to find this out but it's my guess that many losing traders who finally threw in the towel probably didn't realise how close they were to being successful. I was on the verge of packing it in following that day at Ascot but thankfully, I decided to give it one more serious go. The changes I had to make to turn the corner were not massive. Like everyone, I knew I shouldn't chase my losses, take big risks or do any of the other obvious things that cause a bank to blow up. I could have listed all the rules in my sleep; it's textbook stuff which we all know. But following the rules is hard. Really hard. Changing old habits is tricky and overwriting our primitive brain is no easy task. I don't know what it is about humans, but we just have an urge to touch that 'wet paint' even if the sign tells us not to. Perhaps some people need a big loss to give them a metaphorical slap in the face, and in some ways I'm thankful for that big single loss at Ascot as it made me realise that something had to change.

This may sound like something out of one of those dodgy self-help books, but believing in yourself and believing that you can and will become a good trader is essential. You are just as entitled to make money as the next man (or woman). In the past, a lack of confidence in my trading definitely held me back. I'd hear people talking about traders on the exchanges but it didn't feel like they were talking about ME, despite the fact that I was trading quite a lot each week. It was always *someone else* who seemed to be making the money. Even though I was putting in the hours and hard graft, I didn't feel like I was a 'proper' trader (whatever that was). When I'd enter a market to trade, I was scared stiff by these faceless people whom, I was convinced, knew the markets inside out and would eat me up and spit me out. It was always *someone else* who knew which prices would rise or fall and *someone else* who must have a better system or set-up than me.

I'd see big orders in the market and think it must be one of those savvy traders that knew exactly what they were doing. But the fact is the market is made up of thousands of participants, and *the vast majority of those are losing money*. Don't forget that. Fair enough, there are some very good traders out there or perhaps someone with inside information but there's really no need to be scared of the markets. Most of the participants haven't a clue what they are doing either! Keep that in mind when you start to feel inadequate and remember that you have as much right to pick up money as anyone else.

Even when I'd do well, for a while I still felt like a fraud. What if it was just pure luck? Will I be found out? Surely it can't last....

Tell the voice in your head to keep it down and let you trade without interruption. Otherwise, you will fall into the old trap of subconsciously feeling like it is other people who deserve to win. To give you an example of this mentality, I once layed a Gaelic Football team at 3.0 in a lightly traded market, only for the price to come in almost instantly to 2.86 following some very big orders. Rather than accepting the loss and moving on, I got angry with the market and with those faceless traders whom, as I thought, almost certainly knew more than me. 'It's always *someone else* making the money, never me' I told myself. What made it worse was that after I took the loss, the price recovered back to my entry point. Feeling annoyed, I then allowed myself to double up and chase my losses on my next trade. I justified my actions by telling myself that others had an unfair advantage — and that I was entitled to break my own rules *just this once* to recover the money which had 'wrongly' been taken from me. But allowing yourself to break your trading rules because you've been hard done by or to somehow get back at the market will mean you will never, ever become a good trader.

While it's frustrating when it happens, this type of anger at the market is a complete waste of time. The market is not out to get you, nor is it your friend. It is what it is. Getting whipsawed like that is part and parcel of the game and sometimes it actually works in your favour. When it happens now, I just step back and say 'Oh, that's interesting'. I take my loss (or profit) and move on as I understand that these things level out over time. If your washing machine broke down and it cost you £300, you wouldn't get angry and throw your remaining pay packet on a nag down the bookies just to try to win the money back and level out the injustice. Treat your trading capital in the same way. These things happen and the quicker you accept that life isn't fair, the quicker you can become a better trader. Protecting your capital and staying in the game is paramount — no matter how 'unlucky' you've just been. Bad things happen unexpectedly in all aspects of life so why would trading be any different?

It took a while for me to get out of that *someone else* mindset, but when I began making money on a consistent basis, I started to realise that I was finally *becoming that someone else;* the faceless trader I'd feared all those years. And guess what? I'm not a big scary guy who knows the markets inside out with tens of thousands in my account. In fact, I rarely have more than a few grand lodged at any given time and I just look to make small consistent profits when I trade. Sometimes I'll only have a few hundred in my account and I don't live in a flashy house or drive a flashy car, I'm just a normal bloke. I'm no smarter or savvier than the next man; I just made a decision that I'd had enough of reckless trading and all the stress it brings.

If you feel that it's always *someone else* who seems to be making the money, remember that most market participants are losing money. Every time you have a winning trade, remind yourself that you were that *someone else* and another trader has just lost money because of you. Every time you lose a trade, ask yourself if there is anything you could have done differently. If there was, note it down and learn from the experience. If there wasn't, you shouldn't be upset. In fact, you should be happy as it means you've stuck to your set-ups and rules, which in turn means you are on the right road.

A BRIEF HISTORY OF THE BETTING EXCHANGES

Simplicity is the ultimate sophistication — Leonardo da Vinci

IT would be hard to overstate the impact that the exchanges (Betfair in particular) have had on the betting industry and it's definitely true that the punter has never had it so good. The bookie shops you were forced to use if you wanted to place a bet in the pre-Internet days were usually small, smoke-filled little rooms. Even though I used to use them myself, the old bookmaker shops had a bad reputation and alongside genuine racing fans, it's fair to say they attracted their fair share of degenerates. It might be hard to impress on younger readers who grew up using the Internet just how different things were back then. I remember visiting my local bookmakers in the mid 90s trying to put a bet on a rugby match and it took a couple of phone calls to head office before the girl behind the counter could offer me some odds. Indeed, many bookmaker shops offered horseracing and football markets only, and to get a bet on what was considered a minor event such as boxing, snooker, darts or even tennis was often hard to do. When Internet betting became widely available, the bookies were forced to clean up their act in order to attract customers back to the shops and you'd have to say that today, the vast majority are now clean, modern and pleasant places to visit. I reckon there'll always be a future for some sort of bricks and mortar betting shops but as mobile technology advances at a rate of knots, their importance is certainly diminishing.

As much as I love the exchanges, I'd hate to see the offline bookmakers die out completely. There are certain people who don't like giving out their credit card details online, or having to jump through hoops to set up an account so there should always be some sort of market for backers and layers who like to deal in cash. In fact, my wife and I visit Longchamp racecourse occasionally for the Prix de l'Arc de Triomphe and one of the things we dislike about the place is the lack of on-course layers. In France, the racecourses have a pool betting system similar to the old Tote called the Pari-Mutuel where you bet at a counter or through an automated machine

— and we always find that the great atmosphere found in the betting rings of Britain and Ireland is distinctly missing. While the betting rings of Britain and Ireland have become a hell of a lot quieter in recent years, partly due to the exchanges, they add a sense of tradition, occasion and indeed fun to proceedings. In France, it all just seems a little bit soulless. But bookmakers have their downsides and before the exchanges put a spanner in the works, the books often had ridiculous over-rounds, especially on the smaller events. In my view, the lack of large over-rounds is the greatest thing about the exchanges and it's why they continue to grow.

If you are unfamiliar with the concept of an over-round, it's basically the margin the bookmaker takes on a book in order to make money. If you were betting on the toss of a coin for example, the book offered should be 100% as both sides have a 50% chance of winning (50+50=100). However, if a bookmaker were offering a 100% book, he'd never make money over time so instead, he might offer 4/5 on heads and even money on tails.

To work out the implied percentage chance something has of winning, **you convert it to a decimal price then divide it into 100**. So odds of 4/5 on heads become 1.8 in decimal odds; and 100 divided by 1.8 is 55.55%. In that example then, the bookmaker's odds suggest that heads has a 55.55% chance of winning — which is, of course, incorrect. His odds of even money (a 50% chance of winning) on tails are accurate but over the long term, he should make money from anyone who backs on heads. The 55.55% on heads and the 50% on tails makes up a book of 105.55%. So in this case, the over-round is said to be 5.55%.

Books of up to 150% on a horse race were not uncommon and the odds offered on football weren't much better. But when the betting exchanges kicked off, the punter was offered a choice — and many chose to go online where it's not uncommon to see books near 100% on the exchanges. Indeed Betfair and Betdaq actually show you the over-round on the book which is very handy and eliminates the need to do the sums. On the lay side, you also want the book to be as close to 100% as possible but it works the opposite way. The lower the figure is below 100%, the worse value you are getting when laying.

			Select a competition:				Select a match:			

Select a competition: Capital One Cup ▼   Select a match: Aston Villa v Tottenham ▼

Betfair Soccer » Capital One Cup » Aston Villa v Tottenham

Aston Villa v Tottenham   Matched: EUR 257,575 [Refresh]

☐ Going in-play   Live Scores   Form Stats

☑ Back & Lay ☑ Market Depth   More options ▶

Selections: (3)	100.6%		Back	Lay		99%
Aston Villa	3.4 €1789	3.45 €625	3.5 €177	3.55 €440	3.6 €1357	3.65 €2242
Tottenham	2.22 €2363	2.24 €4290	2.26 €1271	2.3 €1937	2.32 €2344	2.34 €1616
The Draw	3.5 €4953	3.55 €5381	3.6 €3836	3.65 €2723	3.7 €6924	3.75 €6170

Figure 1.0 showing the over-round of 0.6% on the back side of a Capital One Cup match between Aston Villa and Tottenham.

LIFT OFF

Betfair was launched on the 9th June 2000 and their first market was the Epsom Oaks. The total amount matched on that event was £3,462 which is miniscule by today's standards but once they got underway, their growth was phenomenal. Of course, the concept wasn't new; it was based on the stock market where people could buy and sell stock and get in and out of their positions as they saw fit. Founders Andrew Black and Edward Wray had some experience in this area but surprisingly, they found it hard to get investment for their new idea. There were a number of other exchanges online at the turn of the century but most had technological problems and Black and Wray knew that if they created a hassle-free and easy to use product, it would catch on. One of the bigger exchanges in the early days was flutter.com which was launched before Betfair in April 2000, but their site proved difficult to use. For example, when a punter went to lay a number of selections, he was faced with an immediate problem: each bet was treated separately, even if it was in the same market. So if you wanted to lay four selections in a given market, you had to have enough in your account to cover the liability for each single bet in your account. With Betfair, you only have to cover the 'worst case scenario' if laying multiple selections. This was a far more sensible model and made Betfair much more attractive to layers.

Betfair also allowed for bets to be partially matched, which was not the case with other exchanges. If you wanted to back a selection on flutter.com with £50 for example, you would have to wait for someone on the other side of the book to take you on for that exact amount. This was totally inflexible. Betfair were streets ahead from a technology point of view and within the space of a couple of years, they bought out flutter.com and then completely dominated the market.

In September 2001, Betdaq was launched by Dermot Desmond, one of Ireland's leading businessmen and that company has grown to become Betfair's biggest rival. Desmond freely admits that their technology was also far behind Betfair in the early days and accepts that it cost him vital market share. For a few years, it seemed that Betdaq was destined to fail as they struggled to pick up customers but to be fair, they stuck out the bad times and have actually started to grow quite big in the past few years. While the liquidity is still significantly smaller than on Betfair, their lower commission rates are attractive.

More recently, Betfair scored two PR own-goals which cost them customers. In September 2008, they introduced the 'Premium Charge' for their more successful customers and even though it only affected a very small proportion of members, it attracted a huge amount of negative press. Then in June 2011, the Premium Charge was increased to 60% for some of its most successful punters, some of which were traders. Again, it only affected a small percentage of users but the idea that you will be punished if you win consistently has taken away from their image as the punter's friend and Betdaq has seen volumes continue to grow. As you may know, bookmakers will close winning accounts or restrict the bet size to very small amounts. Betfair once championed itself as the punter's pal that welcomed winners but with the Premium Charges, it can't really make this claim any longer. But in their defence, it's still the best out there in terms of liquidity and technology and it remains the most popular betting exchange on the Internet.

While most of my trading is done on Betfair, it's good to have a choice and more and more traders I know are now using both exchanges. There are a number of smaller exchanges (such as WBX launched in 2006) which are worth investigating but only Betdaq has come close to becoming a major competitor for Betfair. Betfair floated on the London Stock Exchange on 22nd October 2010 at £13 per share which valued the company at £1.4bn although at the time of writing, the price is now lower at just over £10. In 2013, Betdaq were bought by Ladbrokes for a reported £20m and it is hoped that the takeover will increase competition and inject more liquidity into the markets. In fact, Ladbrokes have now incorporated an exchange section on their website which allows Ladbrokes punters to access the Betdaq markets (via the Ladbrokes website).

All that said, it seems that Betfair are beginning to move away from their roots. In 2012, they launched their 'sportsbook' which is basically a traditional bookmaking site. So when you strike a bet on the sportsbook, you are not betting against another punter — you are simply betting against the company. Personally, I can't see where they are going with this and I think it's a step backwards but it must be making them money or else it wouldn't be so heavily promoted. In fact, they have now made the sportsbook their homepage for first time visitors:

Figure 1.1, Betfair's Irish homepage, which now displays their 'sportsbook'.

In my view, person-to-person betting was what made Betfair unique and trailblazing but they seem intent on promoting the sportsbook. If you click on horseracing, for example, you are now faced with a bookie style page. New users now have to click on 'Go to Exchange' on the top left of the page if they want person-to-person betting. Your cookies on your computer should remember your preferences but just be aware of it if you are using a new computer to place a bet:

Figure 1.2, showing Betfair's recent move towards traditional bookmaking. The 'Go to Exchange' button is circled on the top left.

What the future holds for the betting exchanges is anyone's guess. In Britain and Ireland, we grew up with liberal betting laws so it is strange for us to see some countries, including the US, tighten up their gambling regulations in recent years. Expansion has proved tricky, not just for the exchanges, but for bookmakers too. How big they can grow in the future remains to be seen but one thing is for sure, the exchanges are here to stay. And from a punting and trading point of view, that can only be a good thing as more choice means greater competitiveness.

ABSOLUTE BASICS

The superior man makes the difficulty to be overcome his first interest; success comes only later — Chinese philosopher Confucius (551 BC — 479 BC)

THIS book is mostly aimed at those who have a reasonable level of knowledge of the betting exchanges and as such, I don't want to fill up too much space writing about the absolute basics of trading. If you've never used Betfair or Betdaq before, you should visit the help pages on their websites which explain the concepts in great detail. However, if you have somehow stumbled across this book and are wondering what trading is all about, I'll give a very quick explanation.

BACKING AND LAYING

Until relatively recently, sports betting was a fairly straightforward business. If you backed a football team at 3/1, you could expect to receive £3 in winnings for every £1 staked should your bet be successful — and you would also get your stake back. But the ability to lay a selection changed the industry in a number of ways in the early part of this century and soon after the modern sports trader was born. As most readers will know, betting exchanges display their odds in decimal format; so 3/1 on the exchanges would be presented as 4.0 (to convert from fractional odds to decimal, simply add one).

If you want to back that selection at 4.0, you can still do that and accept your winnings. But it is also possible to put yourself in the bookmaker's shoes and lay the selection if you think it will lose. Laying is quite simple really; just think of the traditional roles reversed. If you lay something, you are like the bookie. If you lay something at 3/1, you owe £3 for every £1 staked if the selection wins the event. If the selection loses, you keep the stake.

Prices on the exchanges are constantly moving so the ability to back one price and lay the same selection at another gives rise to the opportunity to lock in a profit or a free bet regardless of whether the selection wins or loses.

Concept wise, trading on the exchanges is not much different than buying and selling on the stock market. On the stock market, you try to sell shares for a higher price than you bought them at, thus making a profit. On the exchanges, you will be attempting to back at a higher price than you layed at (or lay at a low price first and back at a higher price later) but the intention is the same — to lock in a profit.

EXAMPLE

Figure 2.0

Figure 2.0 shows a Betfair screen shot from a horse race from Southwell on the 5th February 2013. I have backed *Waking Warrior* at 5.5 (9/2) using €100 as my stake. As mentioned elsewhere, my Irish account is in Euros. The green figure beside the horse's name shows how much I will profit by if the bet is successful (€450) while the red figures beside the other horse names show that I would lose (€100) should one of those win the race. At this stage, it's pretty much a traditional back bet.

But later, the price of the horse shortens to 5.2.

Because I backed at 5.5 which is higher than 5.2, I'm now in a good position and have three choices. Firstly, I can leave the bet as it is and hope

Waking Warrior wins. Secondly, I could opt for a free bet on *Waking Warrior* whereby I earn money if the horse wins the race, but lose nothing if it doesn't. Thirdly, I could decide to settle for a small profit no matter which horse wins the race. The first option is self explanatory and is no different than any traditional bet. The second free bet option is an interesting one and is something I use quite regularly. Let me explain:

To use this free bet option, I can simply lay the horse at 5.2 using the same amount that I used to back it, in this case €100. As you can see in figure 2.1, I'm now in a good position:

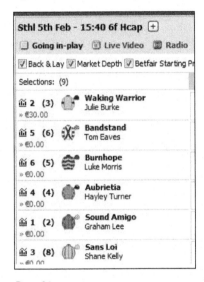

Figure 2.1

If *Waking Warrior* wins, I would gain €450 for the back bet but lose €420 for the lay bet. So the **total profit if the horse wins is €30.**

If *Waking Warrior* loses, I would gain €100 for the lay bet but lose as much for the back bet. So the **total profit if the horse loses is €0.**

In other words, I've a free bet where I get thirty quid if the horse wins but lose nothing if it doesn't win.

The third option, which is the essence of trading, is to lay the selection at a lower price than I backed it at — but with a slightly higher stake, thus guaranteeing a profit no matter which horse wins. Take a look at figure 2.2:

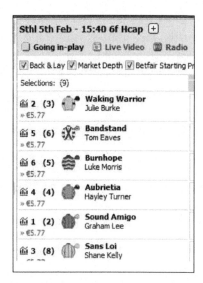

Sthl 5th Feb - 15:40 6f Hcap [+]

☐ Going in-play 📺 Live Video 📻 Radio

☑ Back & Lay ☑ Market Depth ☑ Betfair Starting Pr

Selections: (9)

📊 2 (3) » €5.77		**Waking Warrior** Julie Burke
📊 5 (6) » €5.77		**Bandstand** Tom Eaves
📊 6 (5) » €5.77		**Burnhope** Luke Morris
📊 4 (4) » €5.77		**Aubrietia** Hayley Turner
📊 1 (2) » €5.77		**Sound Amigo** Graham Lee
📊 3 (8)		**Sans Loi** Shane Kelly

Figure 2.2

Having backed *Waking Warrior* at 5.5 with €100, I then lay it with €105.77 when the price drops to 5.2. As you can see here, I will now earn €5.77 no matter which horse wins the race. This is known as a 'green book' as the figure beside each horse's name is coloured green.

In other words:

If *Waking Warrior* wins, I would gain €450 for the back bet but lose €444.23 for the lay bet. So the **total profit if the horse wins is €5.77.**

If *Waking Warrior* loses, I would gain €105.77 for the lay bet but lose €100 for the back bet. So the **total profit if the horse loses is €5.77.**

This is what trading is all about and you can see the appeal of being in a position whereby you earn a fiver on the race no matter what the outcome. And that's before the race has even started. Fair enough, five quid is not all that much but a typical racing day might see five meetings take place with six or seven races on each card so there's potential to make money. In a fast-moving market, how do I know that I need to lay with exactly €105.77 to green up my book? That's where your trading software comes in and thankfully, most programs will have a simple 'green up' button to click so you don't have to do the maths in your head.

Of course we are dealing with positive examples here where the price has moved in our favour, but things are not always so simple in the real world. If the price had drifted after we had placed the initial €100 bet at 5.5, we would have to get out for a loss and the book would be red, which is not such a pretty sight. But taking losses is all part of the game too.

In a high-speed environment, it's not usually practical to use the regular Betfair screen to trade so you need to get some software. Using software will allow you to see the markets in more depth, will allow for one click betting and will generally offer more advanced options. For more on the software options available, see chapter three.

The great thing about trading on the exchanges is that once you complete the trade, your money is immediately available for use again. You don't have to wait until the event is settled before you have access to your funds. This means you can trade the same selection multiple times over, effectively allowing you to leverage your bankroll to quite a high level.

IT ALL ADDS UP

In the above third example, I backed a horse at 5.5 with €100 and later layed it at 5.2 for €105.77. That means my 'turnover' on the trade was €205.77. Let's say I do the same thing again three more times: my total turnover on the race would be over €617. Do I need €617 in my account for this to happen? No. Provided I backed first, I'd only be exposed to losing €100 on any given trade. And, of course, I'm not *actually* exposed to losing €100 on the horse as I'll be trading out before the race starts, rather than letting the bet stand.

Let's take €600 as our ballpark turn over figure on a given race — and assume we turned over a similar amount on every other race that day. If there were five meetings on and each had six races, we would have 30 races to trade. Multiply 30 by €600 and you get €18,000. So from a small bank, you could turn over eighteen grand in a day quite easily.

At that rate, you could turn over a quarter of a million quid in fourteen days, which is a serious amount of money when you think about it. Do you need a quarter of a million quid in your account? Of course not. And that's the whole beauty of trading on the exchanges — you can leverage your money many times over.

So as you can see, turning over your money as much as possible is important — provided, of course, it is done safely and not just for the sake of it. In the financial trading world, you'd need a huge account to turn over those figures but the way the exchanges are set up make it possible for even those with a modest account to turn over considerable sums of money.

LIFE'S NOT FAIR

Some years back, Betfair set up an education team which travelled around Britain and Ireland giving workshops on how to use the exchange to help people make the most of their betting. I attended one of those workshops as a punter in a hotel in Dublin and it proved to be a nice day out with a decent lunch thrown in at Betfair's expense. It's not often one gets the proverbial free lunch and attendance on the day was quite high. At the time, I was writing quite a bit about the exchanges (which were still relatively new) on some online forums and Betfair eventually asked me to help out and become an instructor at their Irish workshops. I was happy to oblige and it was probably the first time I got paid for my expertise. While giving the lectures, we would meet all sorts of punters; high-stakes bookmakers, City traders, students, bored housewives and the typical Joe Punter that likes to stick a tenner on his favourite team of a Saturday.

In the evening sessions, liquid refreshments were provided and one particular winter night sticks out in the mind which involved a rather drunk woman aged about 60. When we got to the part of the evening explaining 'bots' she flipped! (Any kind of trading software was known as a 'bot' back then, which is short for robot). How could the company call itself Betfair, she said, when the availability of bots for certain customers made it completely unfair. She made the point that people using bots had a time advantage, one click betting, trading ladders and loads of other bells and whistles that weren't available to the regular Betfair user. "You should be called Bet-unfair" she insisted as she downed yet another rum and Coke. At this stage, I was getting a bit worried as I was supposed to keep an eye on how much everyone had to drink but I had got distracted while helping another punter. In the meantime, the woman got stuck into the free tab at the bar.

She later calmed down when I agreed to stay back and show her how to get a bot for herself, but the encounter did raise some valid questions about whether or not Betfair (or any other exchange for that matter) is a level playing field. The answer, of course, is that it is most certainly *not* a level playing field and someone, somewhere has better information, better computer speeds, faster pictures, or knows more about the horse or team than you. But just because this is so, it doesn't mean you can't make money too. I would later meet dozens of Betfair users at our education events that would refuse to pay a few pounds a month for a bot out of principle, but think nothing of losing a few hundred from their account over the space of a few weeks. Some of that money may have been saved if they had a bot so it just doesn't make sense to resist on a point of principle. But as they say, there's none so strange as folk.

Whether or not bots are unfair to 'regular' Betfair users is not something to get worked up about. Life isn't fair; it's as simple as that. Is it unfair that the guy who can afford to buy the Racing Post every day has more information than the guy who can only afford a cheap redtop newspaper with basic racecards? Is it unfair that some punters have access to Timeform or other private ratings while others have to rely on widely available free information? In the past ten years, people have become so used to getting information for free on the Internet that they now seem to hold a grudge if someone wants to charge them for something. But if you are going to take this seriously, you need the tools of the trade — and like it or not, a bot is one of them. The fact is, those that pay a small sum to get a bot will have an advantage; so the choice is either to join them, or sit moaning about the injustice of it all. Yes, they cost money but the people who create bots are not a charity and they deserve to be paid for their work — work which gives us traders an advantage over other market participants.

Apart from the speed in placing a bet, one of the biggest advantages a bot gives is the depth of information it offers compared to the regular Betfair screen, particularly with the ladder interface.

THE LADDER
Figure 2.3 shows a race from Doncaster which was held on 7th February 2013, displayed with the regular Betfair screen. If we take a look at the

☐ Going in-play   ☒ Live Video   ☒ Radio   ☒ Tote   ☒ Race Card

☑ Back & Lay ☑ Market Depth ☑ Betfair Starting Price (SP)   More options ▶

Selections: (15)		102.3%		Back	Starting Price		Lay			97.4%
🏠 10 Coverholder — Jonathan England	5 €332	5.1 €230	5.2 €9	SP	SP	5.3 €129	5.4 €35	5.5 €266
🏠 9 Goat Castle — Brian Toomey	6.6 €137	6.8 €50	7 €25	SP	SP	7.2 €33	7.4 €75	7.6 €48
🏠 6 Samtheman — Tom Molloy	8 €4	8.2 €45	8.4 €10	SP	SP	8.8 €9	9 €9	9.2 €11
🏠 5 Marino Prince — Samantha Drake	9.2 €14	9.4 €16	9.8 €398	SP	SP	10.5 €43	11 €2	11.5 €41
🏠 8 Fitandproperjob — Mark Marris	10.5 €112	11 €22	11.5 €220	SP	SP	12 €9	13 €5	14 €3
🏠 2 Mirific — Jeremiah McGrath	10 €241	10.5 €39	11 €43	SP	SP	11.5 €26	12 €44	12.5 €18
🏠 14 Quite Sparky — Edmond Linehan	15.5 €4	16 €116	16.5 €122	SP	SP	17 €25	17.5 €9	18 €17
🏠 Mon Desir	17	17.5	18			19	19.5	20

Figure 2.3

favourite *Coverholder*, we can see that he is trading at 5.2 on the back side and 5.3 on the lay side. At the time the screenshot was taken, there was €9 available on the back side and €129 available on the lay side.

Figure 2.4 also shows *Coverholder*, but this time it is displayed in the ladder format:

You can see the same €9 and €129 available on each side of the book in the

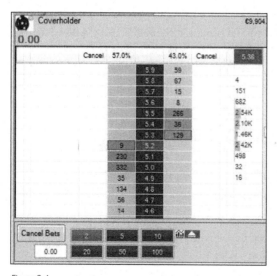

Figure 2.4

respective screenshots but it's simply displayed vertically on the ladder. But you will notice in figure 2.4 that the information regarding the other prices **is not limited to three boxes** as it is on the regular Betfair screen. On the regular Betfair screen, you can only see the prices and money available at 5.0, 5.1 and 5.2 on the back side and 5.3, 5.4 and 5.5 on the lay side. On the ladder, you can see how much is available to back or lay at a glance at all prices ranging from 4.6 to 5.9, with the option to scroll up or down to see even more prices. Not only that, you can place an order at any of those prices at the click of a button. If, for example, I wanted to place an order to back *Coverholder* at 5.7 on the ladder I would simply click the blue box to the right of that price (the box that currently has €15 in it waiting to back).

Something else you will notice is that in the ladder screenshot (figure 2.4), the €9 appears on the pink side of the book and the €129 appears on the blue side of the book, which is the opposite of what is displayed in the regular Betfair screen (figure 2.3). If this is your first time using a ladder, this might seem a little confusing. But remember, the regular Betfair screen is mostly aimed at traditional backers and layers whereas the ladder looks at it from the point of view of those leaving orders or trading.

Let's take that €9 as an example: the regular Betfair screen (figure 2.3) shows the situation from a traditional backer's point of view. It is saying that if you want to back Coverholder at exactly 5.2, you can do so with €9 at the moment. The €9 appears on the blue side as that's how much you can back it with if you are happy to take that price.

But the ladder screen (figure 2.4) shows the situation from the layer's point of view. It is saying that someone has left an order to lay this horse at 5.2 with a €9 stake. So on the ladder, the €9 is displayed on the pink side as it is showing that someone wants to lay at that price.

If you wanted to go ahead and back the horse at 5.2 using the ladder, you would click the blue box (currently blank) opposite the 5.2 price and that would eat away at the €9 on the pink side. It should become clear once you view a few markets but to summarise: the pink side of the ladder is showing all the unmatched lay orders and the blue side is showing all the unmatched back orders.

The ability to place bets at any price you wish with just one click is obviously a huge advantage for trading as it allows you to decide where you want to get in and out. It is far less time-consuming than using the regular Betfair site, in which you have to manually change the odds.

Another great advantage using the ladder is that you can see at a glance how much has been matched at each price in the past. I can see, for example, that €682 has been matched on *Coverholder* at 5.6. We can tell which price has been the most popular (5.5 has 2.54K matched) and what the highest (5.8) and lowest (4.9) prices matched in the past have been. This information can be very useful when trading which we will see in later chapters.

SOFTWARE

Success is the sum of all efforts, repeated day in and day out — bestselling author Robert Collier

TO trade on Betfair or Betdaq, you will need some software. The type of software you require really depends on what type of trader you are so I'm not going to recommend one over the other. There's a vast range of vendors out there, some of which offer free software and some of which offer very advanced products for a monthly fee. A few include both a Betfair and Betdaq product while others offer Betfair only. But a word of caution; fancy software can't turn a bad trader into a good one. If you hand a bad driver the keys to a Porsche, the results are likely to be disastrous. Amongst many other things, software speeds up your trading significantly so make sure you test out each function with minimum stakes or else you will lose your shirt. Understand each function before trying it out — most vendors will offer a user manual or help website when you download the software.

Before you choose, make a list of the functions that you need and then go and look around for free trials and special offers. Ask yourself some questions: do you want to trade with a ladder or a grid? If your trades are normally long-term, can you use the regular Betfair website instead of paying for software? Do you need advanced charts? Ladders? One click betting? Starting out, you will probably require something basic but over time, you may need more advanced options. Personally, I use *Betting Assistant* from Gruss Software which costs me less than €10 per month. I started out with the free version of Gruss and liked the layout and functionality. Also, I've found that the customer service is very good from the guys that run it. In the past, I've also used Bet Angel which is a very decent piece of kit. It has plenty of bells and whistles for the more advanced trader and its founder, Peter Webb, knows the game inside out as he's been trading on the exchanges practically from day one. Peter has put up some videos on YouTube which I've found quite useful. But as I say, I'm not here to recommend one product over another so check out all the options and find one that has functions to suit your style. The following is a list of vendors on the market at the time of writing and some of their key functions. Most have plenty more options available other than the brief descriptions given below — so for more detail on each, visit: http://solutions.betfair.com/

Advanced Cymatic Trader
Includes: one click betting, ladder trading, automated trading etc.

AGT PRO (formerly A Geeks Toy)
Includes: one click betting, ladder trading etc.

Bet Angel Basic (free)
Includes: one click betting, charting, greening up

Bet Angel Professional
Includes: one click betting, ladder trading, automated trading etc.

Bet Ladder for Betfair
Includes: inplay betting, ladder trading, mobile options etc.

Bet-Hedger
Includes: inplay betting, arbitrage etc.

BetDriver
Includes: automated trading, conditional betting, bookmaking etc.

BetGizmo
Includes: one click betting, ladder trading etc.

Betlab
Includes: one click betting etc.

BetOnDroid
Includes: inplay betting, one click betting, ladder trading etc.

Betting Assistant (Gruss Software)
Includes: one click betting, ladder trading, fill or kill etc.

BetTrader Evolution
Includes: one click betting, ladder trading, fill or kill etc.

BFexplorer
Includes: beginner options, one click betting, triggered betting, ladder trading, charting etc.

BotBeetle
Includes: free trading options etc.

Export
Includes: Dutching, calculators etc.

Fairbot
Includes: reverse betting, Dutching, conditional betting etc.

HRFever
Includes: inplay betting, one click betting, triggered betting etc.

JetBet
Includes: one click betting, off-set betting, etc.

MTPro
Includes: live graphs, ladder trading, charting etc.

Smart Market Trader
Includes: inplay betting, one click betting, triggered betting

Traderline
Includes: inplay betting, one click betting etc.

EXPLOITING THE KEY PRICES

'Know your numbers' is a fundamental precept of business — Bill Gates

DO the numbers 2, 3, 4, 6, 10, 20, 30, 50 and 100 mean anything to you? It always amazes me how many Betfair punters, and sometimes even traders, are unaware of how important those numbers are and the difference it can make to their bottom line. I must admit that I was punting on the exchanges for quite some time before I realised their significance. This chapter discusses the 'key prices' on Betfair and why you should rarely, if ever, back at those odds if you are thinking of trading out later.

The above prices are also known as 'crossover points' as they mark changes in the increments in which prices rise or fall on the exchange. By way of illustration, take a look at the ladder in figure 4.0 which shows the price of a football team, currently trading at 2.0:

As you can see, if the odds of the team drop below 2.0, the price moves in ticks of 0.01 with the next prices down being 1.99, 1.98, 1.97 and so on. If the odds rise above 2.0, the price moves in ticks of 0.02 with the next prices up being 2.02, 2.04, 2.06 etc. (Note: a 'tick' simply means a price movement up or down).

This is quite significant. A single move downwards from 2.0 to 1.99 is a change in price of one percent. But a single move upwards from 2.0 to 2.02 is a change in price of two percent. To realise the significance of this, let's assume you are trading and you LAYED this selection at 2.0 using £1000:

- If the price moves *down by one tick* to 1.99, you will lose **£10** on the trade
- If the price moves *up by one tick* to 2.02, you will win **£20** on the trade

2.20
2.18
2.16
2.14
2.12
2.10
2.08
2.06
2.04
2.02
2.00
1.99
1.98
1.97
1.96
1.95
1.94
1.93
1.92
1.91
1.90

Figure 4.0

So as you can see, you are winning £20 per tick each

time the price moves in your favour but only losing £10 per tick each time the price moves against you. By being a layer at 2.0, you have immediately put the odds in your favour. As you have probably worked out by now, the opposite is also true. Let's assume for a moment that you had BACKED the selection at 2.0 using £1000:

- If the price moves *down by one tick* to 1.99, you will earn **£10** on the trade
- If the price moves *up by one tick* to 2.02, you will lose **£20** on the trade

This is why you should never be a backer at those prices; you would lose twice as much per tick should the trade go against you than you would earn should the trade go in your direction. It's a similar situation with the other key prices mentioned earlier. Be aware that:

From **1.01 to 2.0**, prices move in increments of 0.01 (1.02, 1.03, 1.04 and so on).
From **2.0 to 3.0**, prices move in increments of 0.02 (2.02, 2.04, 2.06 and so on).
From **3.0 to 4.0**, prices move in increments of 0.05 (3.05, 3.10, 3.15 and so on).
From **4.0 to 6.0**, prices move in increments of 0.10 (4.10, 4.20, 4.30 and so on).
From **6.0 to 10.0**, prices move in increments of 0.20 (6.20, 6.40, 6.60 and so on).
From **10.0 to 20.0**, prices move in increments of 0.50 (10.5, 11.0, 11.5 and so on).
From **20.0 to 30.0**, prices move in increments of 1.00 (21.0, 22.0, 23.0 and so on).
From **30.0 to 50.0**, prices move in increments of 2.00 (32.0, 34.0, 36.0 and so on).
From **50.0 to 100.0**, prices move in increments of 5.00 (55.0, 60.0, 65.0 and so on).
From **100.0 to 1000.0**, prices move in increments of 10.0 (110.0, 120.0, 130.0 and so on).

Price below	Crossover	Price above
1.99	**2.00**	2.02
2.98	**3.00**	3.05
3.95	**4.00**	4.10
5.90	**6.00**	6.20
9.80	**10.00**	10.5
19.5	**20.00**	21.0
29.0	**30.00**	32.0
48.0	**50.00**	55.0
95.0	**100.00**	110.0

Figure 4.1

As a quick reference, the chart in figure 4.1 shows the crossover points and the prices immediately below/above:

So as pointed out, it is always better to be a layer at those key prices than a backer if you are planning on trading out later. It is also worth noting that these prices can become significant areas of resistance (difficult to break through). When people realise the importance of the crossover points, they will obviously want to become a layer rather than a backer. And if there are more layers than backers at a given price, the backers won't be able to break through it.

This is why you often see steamers (selections whose price is dropping rapidly) come to an abrupt halt when they hit a key price; there is simply too much layer money in the way and the backers can't break through it. If a steamer does break through a key price and continues to drop, take note, especially in a heavily traded market. Usually, it takes a significant amount of backer money to smash through a key price so when it happens, it's an indicator that there is serious money supporting the selection.

Before we look at how to make money from the key prices, let's take a look at an example of how these prices often prove to be strong areas of resistance. Figure 4.2 shows the win odds for *Newcastle United* in a recent Premier League game. This screenshot was taken the evening before the match so liquidity was still relatively low but nonetheless, it's an excellent example of the struggle between backers and layers at one of the key prices.

Figure 4.2

When the market opens, the price zigzags up and down for a short time before settling around 3.15. While the price briefly touched 3.75, this fluctuation early on is normal as the market tries to find its level and usually involves very small sums of money. For trading purposes, ignore these early fluctuations. Take a look at the horizontal price line at 3.0. As you can see, the backers try numerous times to push the price below that line but each time they get there, the price bounces back slightly. As mentioned, it's never good to be a backer at 3.0 so when the price comes down to this level, the layers who know about the key price concept enter the market. In any market, if the layers outnumber the backers the price should rise so hence the bounce every time the price hits 3.0.

Further on, you can see a price spike up to 3.50 following some negative team injury news. It didn't stay long at 3.50 and very soon, those persistent backers had pushed the price back down to try break the 3.0 line once again. The line is tested a number of times before the backers finally get the message and the price settles just under 3.25.

HOW CAN WE MAKE MONEY FROM THE KEY PRICES?

As usual, it's all about timing. You need to get your lay order in at the key price early so that your money is at the top of the queue when the backers start to test the price. That said, it's a bit of a balancing act as you should avoid markets where there is little or no liquidity, as the prices will be unstable in such markets and often zigzag.

EXAMPLE ONE

Figure 4.3 shows the win odds for *Blackburn Rovers* in a match they weren't fancied to win. The screenshot was taken about 8 a.m. on the morning of the match (kick off was at 3 p.m.).

	8.20	19
	8.00	50
	7.80	223
	7.60	101
	7.40	14
	7.20	67
	7.00	210
22	6.80	
87	6.60	
7	6.40	
22	6.20	
202	6.00	
8	5.90	

Figure 4.3

Blackburn are trading around 7.0. The nearest key price is 6.0. While the market is not hugely robust at this time of the day, there's a couple of hundred on each side of the book which should stop any wild price swings. At 6.0, you will notice that there is £202 in the pink box waiting to lay. Some trader(s) probably had the same idea as me and got in early. However, I'm still happy to put in a lay order at 6.0 and get behind that £202. As we get nearer to kick-off, thousands will be traded on both sides of the book so £202 ahead of me in the queue should not become a problem. I'm trading with £100 so I click the pink button at 6.0 and my order is fired in.

I must now decide how many ticks profit I will take if the trade is successful and I must also decide at what point I'm going to get out at should the trade go wrong. I'm only looking to get a couple of ticks profit out of this trade so if my lay is matched at 6.0, I'll take my profit if or when the price rises two ticks to 6.4. Should the trade go against me, I'll get out for a two tick loss at 5.8. As mentioned, because 6.0 is a crossover price, I'll earn more from the two tick win if the trade is successful than I would lose from the two tick loss should the trade go against me. If the price never drops down to 6.0, that's fine as I can just cancel my order with no money lost or won.

Figure 4.4 shows the same market an hour before kick-off. The price has drifted down to 6.0 but it is finding it hard to break through — there is a wall of money at that price (over £4,000) as traders try to lay the crossover. A few hundred is getting matched at 6.0 every few minutes but it keeps bouncing back to 6.2. Because I got in early, my £100 has already been matched at this stage. Once my money was matched, I placed my exit orders. As you can see, one is at 6.4 in case the trade is successful and the other is at 5.8 in case the trade goes wrong:

		6.80	885		
		6.60	1093		
		6.40	786	100	
		6.20	1118		
	4096	6.00			
	332	5.90			
100	441	5.80			
	2471	5.70			
	1569	5.60			

Figure 4.4

At this point, I have a lay on *Blackburn* open at 6.0 and I have my exit points set up; so now it's just a matter of hoping the backers can't break through the key price and that it takes a bounce up to 6.4. If the backers do push through 6.0, I have my stop-loss in place at 5.80. But because the prices move in bigger increments above 6.0, I will earn more from the two ticks should the trade be successful than I would lose from the two ticks should the trade go against me.

EXAMPLE TWO

This is actually an example of a market that should be avoided. Figure 4.5 shows the win odds for a horse in a good quality race roughly five minutes before the off time. This market is fairly robust with plenty of money on both sides of the book:

	3.25	3691
	3.20	7894
	3.15	11231
	3.10	10256
	3.05	12243
14356	3.00	
226	2.98	
589	2.96	
1004	2.94	
2589	2.92	
1127	2.90	

Figure 4.5

The horse is trading at 3.0 which is a crossover price but note that there's already £14,356 in the queue waiting to lay at that price. If you put in an order now, you would have to wait until the backers had taken all of that money before your order gets matched. Then you have to hope that the price bounces back. But think about it; if the backers are willing to eat away over £14,000, they must mean business and may well be about to break down through the 3.0 barrier. Do you really want to risk getting in late during a possible breakdown in price? The back (light blue) side of this book is already looking strong and has a good deal of money pushing down — so that 3.0 may not hold. In this case, it may be worth waiting to see if the price breaks through 3.0 and if so, back the horse at 2.98 in the hope of catching a downward trend (with a stop-loss set around 3.05). Otherwise, just stay away — you've missed the boat. Don't get upset or hung up about it, there'll be plenty of other opportunities later. Novice traders get angry when they miss an opportunity and often jump in late anyway, much to the detriment of their balance. Don't get angry with the market, it's just a numbers game. Professionals know that there's always tomorrow, next week and next month. Only trade when conditions are in your favour and be sure to control the risk on each trade.

SUMMARY

This strategy is all about knowing your numbers. In the above examples, I've used Betfair but similar opportunities exist on Betdaq (although the crossover points are slightly different). You may wonder why people would still be backers at the key prices but the reality is that a lot of traditional punters don't take much notice of the price increments. Plus, traditional punters are drawn to round numbers; people like to back at 2/1 or 3/1 as they are familiar looking odds and it's easy for them to work out their potential winnings. This is why it still works. You can see this in the world of financial trading too where round numbers can become significant areas of support and resistance in some markets.

A traditional football punter might decide that he wants to back his team at 2/1 and thinks he is being smart by insisting that he won't take any less. He then logs on to Betfair and sees the price at 3.0 (2/1). Happy days! He'll go ahead and back the selection at 3.0, totally unaware that it's a key price for us traders. In some ways, we need the casual punters that are not too bothered investigating things like price increments. It pleases me when I see Betfair and Betdaq spending money on advertising trying to attract the casual punter as it means that there should be more opportunities in the future for traders to exploit the key prices.

One of the most important things to do is decide on your entry and exit points and make sure you stick to them once your trade is executed. Remember, nothing is foolproof and you often get breakouts. Like every strategy, this type of trade doesn't always work but it puts the odds slightly in your favour so you can be wrong more than you are right and still make some money.

FILLING THE GAPS
(SCALPING PART ONE)

He that can have patience can have what he will — Benjamin Franklin

SCALP trading, or 'scalping' as it's known in the business, involves getting in and out of markets quickly and often, only taking a tick or two profit per trade. Because the profit levels are so small, scalpers need to complete a high number of trades per day to make it worthwhile. Scalpers are not after the big price moves; they just want to get their money in and out of the market as many times as possible.

When I first heard about scalp trading, I thought it sounded like an easy way to make a quick buck but like most things in this game, it's not quite as simple as it seems. Initially, I would try to predict which way the market would move and then take a position accordingly. If I thought the price was going to rise, I'd lay first and then try to back at a tick or two higher and if I thought the price was going to fall, I'd back first and then try to lay off my bet if I was correct. While this approach netted me plenty of successful trades, the winning trades were not earning enough to cover the losing ones and when my starting bank of a monkey (£500) had dwindled down below £50 over the space of six months, I finally admitted defeat. I was frustrated in the extreme and couldn't work out why I was losing money but looking back, my entry points were purely based on guesswork and I do admit that my stakes were probably too large. I was trying to predict which way the market would move which is what most traders try to do — but this is completely the wrong approach to scalping and it's also the reason why so many people lose money. A few months later I was sitting at home watching a very lightly-traded market for an all-weather seller when a few ideas dawned on me. It sounds paradoxical, but I became a good scalp trader when I realised that you don't need to know which way the market is going to move in order to make money. Let me explain....

As discussed elsewhere, a lack of liquidity in any given market can make life difficult for traders. Obviously, the bigger horseracing events such as the Cheltenham Festival and Royal Ascot are going to attract plenty of backers and layers and hence the markets will be very robust. But what about a wet Wednesday afternoon at Wolverhampton? Let's be honest, the day-to-day meetings are not always top-drawer stuff. The fare on offer, particularly midweek, can be poor to put it kindly. Some of these markets only come alive a few minutes before the off and it can be mind-numbingly boring watching a chart or ladder which is practically standing still with very little money on each side of the book. However, these quiet periods can offer opportunities for those that have a little patience, and this 'filling the gaps' strategy actually uses the lack of liquidity as an opportunity to make money.

This strategy involves one tick scalping, and the thing I love is that you don't have to try to predict which way the market will go. You simply find a good spot to put in an initial order, then wait patiently for the price to move your way. If the price doesn't move in your direction, you can cancel the trade with no damage done. This strategy allows you to get ahead of the queue thus ensuring a good fill rate with your trades. It actually works the opposite way to most regular trades in that you pick your exit point first in this strategy.

EXAMPLE ONE

Figure 5.0 shows the ladder for *Layla's Boy*, which was running in a low-value maiden race. The market wasn't particularly strong early on and this screenshot was taken roughly eight minutes before the race went off.

As mentioned earlier, you should always compose yourself before you trade, and take a few moments to take in what the market is telling you. So what can we tell from a quick glance at this ladder?

Firstly, we can tell that the current price of *Layla's Boy* is 3.30.

Secondly, we can tell that it's not a particularly strong favourite right now. A quick scan of the light-blue (back) column and also the pink (lay) column reveal that there is more money queued up to lay the horse than there is queued up to back it. While we don't necessarily need to know which way the market is going to move in order to trade this horse, it's more likely to drift if the money on the back side remains thin on the ground.

Thirdly, we can tell that no-one has an order in to back the horse at 3.65 as the light-blue box beside that price is empty. **This forms the basis for**

	3.80	8
	3.75	269
	3.70	49
	3.65	
	3.60	42
	3.55	12
	3.50	63
	3.45	104
	3.40	45
	3.35	189
	3.30	89
62	3.25	
323	3.20	
420	3.15	
223	3.10	
101	3.05	
433	3.00	
620	2.98	
120	2.96	
98	2.94	
104	2.92	

Figure 5.0

our trade and 3.65 will be our exit point later on. The trick here is to get ahead of the queue by putting in a back order at 3.65 while the box is empty (as we will attempt to lay later on at 3.60). If you spot an empty box (a gap) in the market like this, follow these steps:

1. Put in an order to back the horse at 3.65. In this case, I used £100 as the stake. Be careful to use stakes that the market can easily absorb. £1,000, for example, would be completely out of place in this market and other traders would spot you a mile away. As you can see in figure 5.1, the light-blue box beside 3.65 is no longer empty as it is now displaying my unmatched £100 back order.

	3.80	8	
	3.75	269	
	3.70	49	
	3.65	100	100
	3.60	42	
	3.55	12	
	3.50	63	
	3.45	104	
	3.40	45	
	3.35	189	
	3.30	89	
62	3.25		
323	3.20		
420	3.15		
223	3.10		
101	3.05		
433	3.00		
620	2.98		
120	2.96		
98	2.94		
104	2.92		

Figure 5.1

2. At this point, it's just a matter of playing the waiting game. This is where the aforementioned patience comes into play. We are now going to sit and watch the market and wait on the price to drift up to 3.60, which is just below our order. If the price doesn't rise, that's OK; we can scratch the trade at any time at no cost.

3. Figure 5.2 was taken about five minutes later. As hoped, the price has now drifted up and is just below our order. Note that the market is now a lot more liquid as we approach the off and there is £554 in the queue waiting to back the horse at 3.65, £100 of which is mine. Crucially, I know that *my money is first in the queue* to back the horse at 3.65 as that box was empty when I put in my order earlier on.

		3.80	2452	
		3.75	1008	
		3.70	869	
		3.65	554	100
		3.60	20	
	788	3.55		
	302	3.50		
	425	3.45		
	869	3.40		

Figure 5.2

4. As the price rises, keep an eye on the money in the light-blue box at 3.60. Have your mouse at the ready — when that money starts to get eaten away, it's time to put in your lay. In figure 5.2, there is only £20 left so now is a good time for me to click the pink box and lay at 3.60.

5. I click on the pink box at 3.60 using £100 and my lay order is submitted. I now have a back order for £100 at 3.65 and a lay order at 3.60. Figure 5.3 shows that £20 has been matched from my lay order (leaving £80 to be matched), while £10 has matched from my back order (leaving £90 to be matched). I'm now in an excellent position. My money is at the top of the queue on **both sides of the book** and I can be very confident that I will be quickly matched at both prices.

		3.80	2231	
		3.75	983	
		3.70	812	
		3.65	623	90
80	241	3.60		
	790	3.55		
	241	3.50		
	385	3.45		

Figure 5.3

6. The rest of my order gets matched within seconds and the trade is successful.

So where does that leave me now?

- If *Layla's Boy* wins the race: I'll earn £265 from the back bet at 3.65, but lose £260 from the lay bet at 3.60. **Total = £5**
- If *Layla's Boy* loses the race: I'll lose £100 from the back bet at 3.65, but earn £100 from the lay bet at 3.60. **Total = £0**

In other words, I'll earn a fiver if the horse wins the race but I won't lose any money if it doesn't. I also have the option of greening up (discussed earlier) so I can profit no matter which horse actually wins. Fair enough, a fiver is not a huge amount of money but it only took me minutes to do this and scalping is all about turning your money over as much as possible. Pennies make pounds as they say, and it all adds up. You can also increase your stakes over time to earn more money as you gain experience and confidence.

EXAMPLE TWO

Meetings Man was trading around 11.0 in a handicap, roughly five minutes before the start of the race. There was a reasonable amount of liquidity on that horse but there are still some gaps we can exploit.

In the previous example, we found an empty price box which ensured our order was first in the queue. In this case, there are no empty price boxes (which is not ideal), but there are a number of prices with very little money beside them so it is still possible to get some scalp trades in. Have a look at the pink and light-blue columns in Figure 5.4. On the lay side, there is only £8 in the queue at 9.20. On the back side, there is only £14 in the queue at 14.50.

So in this example, I actually have an opportunity to put in orders on both sides of the book. I immediately put in an order to lay at 9.20 and another order to back at 14.50, this time using £50 as my stake (figure 5.5). As mentioned, this differs from the first example because I'm not quite first in the queue; but small sums such as £8 and £14 ahead of me should not prove troublesome.

Figure 5.4

Bid	Price	Offer
	16.00	78
	15.50	122
	15.00	48
	14.50	14
	14.00	22
	13.50	97
	13.00	154
	12.50	199
	12.00	345
	11.50	287
	11.00	
121	10.50	
147	10.00	
98	9.80	
47	9.60	
209	9.40	
8	9.20	
143	9.00	
198	8.80	
54	8.60	
22	8.40	

Figure 5.5

	Bid	Price	Offer	
		16.00	78	
		15.50	122	
		15.00	48	
		14.50	64	50
		14.00	22	
		13.50	97	
		13.00	154	
		12.50	199	
		12.00	345	
		11.50	287	
		11.00		
	121	10.50		
	147	10.00		
	98	9.80		
	47	9.60		
	209	9.40		
50	58	9.20		
	143	9.00		
	198	8.80		
	54	8.60		
	22	8.40		

In figure 5.5, you can see that my two orders have been placed, and my money brings the amount waiting to lay at 9.20 to £58 (my £50 plus the £8 already ahead of me). Similarly, my back order at 14.50 brings the total amount of money waiting to back at that price to £64. It's now a matter of playing the waiting game. I can't repeat this often enough: the great thing about this strategy is that we don't have to predict which way the price will go. We have orders on both sides of the book so we can just sit and wait.

As it happens, the price of the horse drops down over the next two minutes. In figure 5.6, the price is trading at 9.60, close to my lay order at 9.20:

		11.00	1047	
		10.50	878	
		10.00	505	
		9.80	459	
	47	9.60		
	322	9.40		
50	400	9.20		
	444	9.00		
	120	8.80		

Figure 5.6

At this point, I have my finger on the mouse and I'm getting ready to back at 9.40. When I see the money getting eaten away at that price (the pink box which contains £322 at present), I will click the light-blue back button. You can see that there is now £400 looking to lay the horse at 9.20 but I'm happy in the knowledge that I'm up near the top of that queue with just £8 ahead of me.

Quite quickly, the price came down to 9.40 and I backed (using £50). At this point, I was very near the top of the queue on both sides of the book and my orders were filled within seconds. This was an interesting case as only around £80 was matched at 9.20 and then the price started to rise again. Thankfully, £50 of the £80 matched was mine; **I was up at the top of the queue** because I took my position early. So you can see why getting in early is crucial. Had I been at the back of that £400, my money would not have been matched and the trade would have been a loser or breakeven at best.

As the off time approached, I cancelled my earlier back order at 14.5, happy to have completed one good trade.

So where do I stand at this point?

- If *Meetings Man* wins the race: I'll earn £420 from the back bet at 9.4, but lose £410 from the lay bet at 9.2. **Total = £10.**
- If *Meetings Man* loses the race: I'll lose £50 from the back bet at 3.65, but earn £50 from the lay bet at 3.60. **Total = £0**

WHAT CAN GO WRONG?

On occasion, you can open a trade but then find that the market moves against you immediately and never touches your initial order. If this happens, you must get out for a one or two tick loss straight away. Remember, a successful trade will only earn you one tick at a time so this is certainly not a strategy where you leave a bad trade open and hope for the best. Be clinical. The trade either works or it doesn't and once active, it shouldn't last more than a few seconds. If you've entered a trade and the price is going against you, get out of the trade without hesitation. Scalping is all about getting quick small profits as often as possible so when you have a losing trade, you must get out ASAP as the margins are extremely tight. If you have problems getting out of bad trades, set an automatic stop-loss (discussed later). Another common error is actually entering the trade too early, often caused through 'butter fingers'. Sometimes it can be difficult to sit for long periods with your finger ready on the mouse, waiting for the money to get eaten away near your price. A quick slip of the finger has often resulted in my bet going in too early and when this happens, the only option is to get out immediately. When scalping, never EVER leave a bad trade open and hope for the best. Remember, if you lose five ticks on a single bad trade because you refused to get out for a loss, you will need to have five successful trades in a row just to get back to even. Don't put that pressure on yourself. Take it from me — I've been there before and lost the money. Letting bad trades ride is just pure gambling, and trading is not supposed to be about gambling. Just accept some small losses along the way; it's part and parcel of the game. No strategy will work 100% of the time and the sooner you accept this, the sooner you will become a good trader.

This is one of my favourite types of trade, mainly because you don't have to predict which way the market will move. You simply look for gaps in the prices, fill them, and then wait for the market to do its thing. If the market never moves in your direction, that's fine too and you can simply cancel the trade with no money lost. The difference between this approach and regular trading is that you are actually setting your exit point first, and the entry point follows on later, should the market move in your direction. While the profits involved are quite small, it can have a very high success rate and with a bit of patience, you should find dozens of opportunities each day.

QUICKFIRE TRADING (SCALPING PART TWO)

I believe the true road to preeminent success in any line is to make yourself master of that line — Scottish-American industrialist, Andrew Carnegie

As a kid, my older brother was very interested in Native American culture so the first time I heard the word 'scalping', it was in relation to the horrific practice of removing the scalp from someone's head — sometimes while that person was still alive. The second time I heard of scalping was during the European Soccer Championships in 1988 when my father tried in vain to get my brother and I tickets for one of the Ireland matches. "I can't get any tickets" he explained, "the effing scalpers have bought them all up and are charging an arm and a leg for them". There was a sense of hatred in his voice and I actually think he would agree with the description of 'scalping' offered on the not so politically correct *Urban Dictionary* website:

> *Scalping: someone who purchases large quantities of goods (usually tickets) early with the sole intention of re-selling them at a higher price at a later date (closer to the event)....The absolute scum of the earth, worse than neo-Nazis, telemarketers, and rapists combined. They lack the decency, intelligence and integrity to make an honest living, so they prey upon and exploit other people's love of music, sport and general interests.*

OK then. So who wants to be a scalper?

Thankfully, scalpers are not held with such disdain in the trading world although there are a significant amount of exchange users which, for reasons known to themselves, don't welcome traders with open arms. Without traders, the markets would be far less liquid so anytime someone starts moaning about what I do, I switch off and don't listen to their nonsense. Liquidity (the amount of money available to back and lay) drives the markets. As explained in the previous chapter, scalpers only make a tick or two profit per trade (unlike our ticket selling friends) and need to get in and out as quick as possible. For those that have good hand-eye coordination and like the cut and thrust of a fast-moving market, it may be worth trying out this second scalping strategy to see if you can make a few quid out of it. Not everyone is cut out to be a scalper and different readers will get different results. I've shown this strategy to a number of people before and for some people, it just clicks while others get themselves into a panic and lose money. I guess it depends on your temperament and you'll have to try it out with small stakes to see if you can make it work. I've only ever tried it on horseracing markets — if you find that it works on other sports, please fire me an email with details.

Firstly, try to find a relatively stable market where the prices are not fluctuating wildly. This strategy will not work in volatile markets. Any market can change quite quickly depending on conditions but very generally speaking, my experience has found that:

- Races of high liquidity are stable
- High quality races are stable
- Small fields are volatile
- Large field with short priced favourite are volatile
- Large field with a weak favourite are steady

Mostly, I'll just trade the favourite although if conditions are suitable, I'll also work the second favourite too.

Once you've found a steady market, the next thing to do is check the WOM (weight of money) percentages on the selection you are trading (for more on WOM, see chapter 12). Depending on your software, you may need to click a button in order for this indicator to display. This indicator measures the amount of money waiting to back or lay the selection. The bigger the WOM on any given side, the more chance there is that the selection's price will move in that direction. For example, if the WOM was 80% on the back side and 20% on the lay side, the selection is likely to shorten as there are a lot of people looking to back.

EXAMPLE

In this strategy, we are looking for horses where the WOM is relatively even on each side. In figure 6.0, you can see that the WOM is 54% on the back side and 46% on the lay side. These figures can change quite quickly so speed is of the essence. In a perfect world, the WOM would be 50% on each side — although anywhere up to a 60/40 percent split should be OK.

WOM		WOM
46%		54%
	2.74	560
	2.72	470
	2.70	628
	2.68	1101
	2.66	1297
	2.64	1368
1250	2.62	
1085	2.60	
899	2.58	
641	2.56	
179	2.54	
590	2.52	

Figure 6.0

The next thing to check is that there is a reasonable amount of money available on both sides of the book in the immediate back and lay prices available. Again, going back to figure 6.0, you can see that there is £1,368 available on the back side, and £1,250 available on the lay side. We will be taking a position on both sides of the book — and we need the levels of money available on each side to be similar amounts. If, for example, there was £3,000 on the back side and £400 on the lay side, this would be far too lopsided to trade. Again, in an ideal world, the amount available on each side would be exactly the same but in reality, this rarely happens. In this case, £1,368 and £1,250 are not too far off each other — this means that when we put in our order, there will be a similar amount of money ahead of us in the queue on each side.

Next, put in your order on both sides of the book — that is, put in an order to **back the horse at 2.64** and another order to **lay the horse at**

2.62. We are only looking to earn one tick. Because we choose a steady market that had similar pressure on both the back and lay side, we can be relatively confident that the backers and layers will chip away at both sides, eventually hitting our two orders.

We now sit and wait for both orders to get matched. The key three points to remember are:

1. Only place your order in a relatively steady market. A market with wild swings may run away from you after one order was matched. Be sure to check the charts to see the historical data. Avoid selections that are fluctuating greatly in price!

2. Before you place your orders, wait for the WOM to be relatively similar on both the back and lay sides. This helps to ensure you are not backing or laying a steamer or a drifter.

3. Only put in your orders if there is a decent amount of money on BOTH the back and lay sides. The levels of money available should be relatively similar.

WHAT CAN GO WRONG?

Of course, it all looks pretty simple on paper here but in reality, the market will be moving quite quickly and the WOM will be changing constantly. Your window of opportunity may only last a few seconds. There's always the chance that some big market player(s) will get involved and your beautifully balanced market will become lopsided as quick as a flash. That happens — we can never truly predict the market and beginners can protect themselves by using stop-losses for when it does occur. If the book percentages change to make the market lopsided and your order hasn't yet been matched, cancel your orders.

The above are guidelines only — I'll often adapt the rules slightly for different markets and you may wish to add some rules of your own. For example, I won't place a bet unless there is at least £300 available on both the back and lay side (I sometimes go higher on bigger races). If there are only small amounts available, it's much easier for single traders/bettors to manipulate the market. We want to focus on robust markets with people punting on both sides of the book as these are the markets that are likely to remain steady. Also, if I find that one order has been taken but the other seems to be stalling, I will move my order up or down and try to get out at breakeven point. Your orders should be getting matched roughly the same time (as they had roughly the same amount of money in front of them in the queue) and if you find yourself waiting on one, it could be a sign to get out as the market is moving away from you. Finally, I like to put in a stop-loss of about 3-4 ticks in this strategy, just in case the market takes an unexpected swing and starts steaming or drifting in a certain direction. However the use of a stop loss does not mean I won't get out earlier if I feel the trade is not working.

Like the scalping strategy mentioned earlier, this is one of my favourite ways to trade simply because you don't have to predict which way the market will go. You just wait for conditions to be right, and then you strike. There are plenty of opportunities to scalp in this way on most races although I must emphasise again that you must be quick off the draw. If you dislike sitting staring at the screen, it may not be for you but with a little bit of patience, there's decent money to be made.

SUPPORT AND RESISTANCE TRADING

History doesn't repeat itself, but it does rhyme — Mark Twain

ONE of the main themes of this book is that you don't have to predict which way the market will move to be a good trader. Markets are generally random and you must enter every trade with the understanding that almost anything can happen. But that said, people are creatures of habit and don't like to stray too far from the crowd so in certain markets, we can take an educated guess at how far the masses will let a price travel in either direction. In the financial world, the strategy described in this chapter is often referred to as the 'bouncing ball' and it seeks to find the key levels of support and resistance around a selection's price. The best way to understand this strategy is to think of a ping-pong ball bouncing up and down in a room: if the ball drops to the floor, it will bounce off it and rise back up. If the ball hits the ceiling, it will bounce off it and come down. That's the basis for this strategy.

EXAMPLE ONE

Figure 7.0 shows the activity of a price over the space of twenty minutes and you can see that the selection has been trading in a range between 2.30 and 2.40:

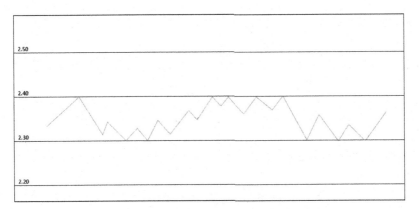

Figure 7.0

In this case, 2.30 is the 'floor' and 2.40 is the 'ceiling' because each time the price hits one of those levels, it bounces back off it. Traders can make a profit here by backing at 2.40 or laying at 2.30 and then exiting their trade for a couple of ticks profit following the price bounce.

Before you place your order, always make sure that both the floor and ceiling prices have been tested a number of times to ensure they are solid areas of support and resistance. Here, both the 2.30 and the 2.40 price have been tested five times each so far. We've no idea if the price is going to rise or fall right now — but we can give an educated guess that it will bounce off either the floor or ceiling, whichever way it moves.

Why does it bounce? It's all about the battle between the backers and the layers, and how each perceives a value bet. In this case, the price is occasionally allowed to rise but only to a certain point (2.40). When the price rises to 2.40, the backers think 'hey, that's not a bad bet' and they step in and back the selection, thus putting downward pressure on the price. Similarly, the price is only allowed to drop to a certain point before it becomes attractive to the layers. The layers are interested in taking on this selection anytime it hits 2.30. Once they start laying, it puts upward pressure on the price. This battle between backers and layers continues for a time and the price bounces between the support and resistance lines. Often, the battle between backer and layer can be extremely tight, but in this case they've left us a nice gap in between the prices they are willing to take. While the backers and layers play their game of tug-of-war, the traders make some money in the price gap between 2.30 and 2.40. This in-between area is pretty much no-man's land. There will be bets struck in no-man's land but it's clear that the big backers want the selection at 2.40 while the big layers want to take it on at 2.30.

If we go to the ladder view in figure 7.1, you can see that the price of the selection is currently trading at 2.36, somewhere in between the floor and the ceiling. You can also see that I have two £100 orders; one to back the selection in case the price hits the ceiling, and one to lay in case the price hits the floor.

This is a form of scalp trading so I'm only seeking to get a couple of ticks profit from the trade. Again, timing is important and you don't want to put

		2.42	145	
		2.40	520	100
		2.38	18	
	355	2.36		
	498	2.34		
	260	2.32		
100	452	2.30		
	120	2.28		

Figure 7.1

your order in too late as you'll have too much money ahead of you in the queue. But it's a double-edged sword in some ways as you have to wait until the floor and ceiling have been tested a number of times before you put in your order (as you need to be sure the support and resistance areas are solid). So at times, you might need to accept that there will be *some* money ahead of you in the queue.

Figure 7.2 shows the betting a few moments later:

		2.44	120	
		2.42	149	
		2.40	774	
	51	2.38		
100	223	2.36		
	271	2.34		
	89	2.32		
100	640	2.30		

Figure 7.2

The price has risen to 2.40 and my back order has been matched. I'm now waiting on the price to bounce back down, and in preparation for that bounce, I've put in a lay order at 2.36 which will earn me a two tick profit. Sometimes the bounce can happen quite quickly so you may wish to use the 'tick offset' function if you are not so fast with the mouse. The tick offset function can be found on most types of trading software and places a counter trade or exit point as soon as the trade is opened. You will also notice that I've left my original lay order at the floor price of 2.30 in case the price comes down to the floor later on. In this case, the price came down to 2.34 which successfully completed the trade.

BREAKOUTS

In a perfect world, prices would bounce off the floor and ceiling every single time and I'd be sitting in the south of France somewhere sipping fine wine while counting my dough. But it's never that simple of course, and traders must be prepared for a breakout. Again, using the ping-pong ball analogy, sometimes the ball can be travelling so strongly that it smashes up through the ceiling to the next floor (or breaks through the floor and ends up in the basement).

Figure 7.3 shows a breakout:

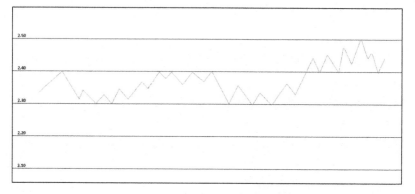

Figure 7.3

Having traded in a range for some time, the layers decided they wanted to oppose this selection with some serious money, and the strength of that money has sent the price smashing through the ceiling at 2.40. This is known as a breakout. Once we have a breakout, we must now wait and see if the market will find a new floor and ceiling. Quite often (but not always), you will find that the old ceiling price can become the new floor price and that's what has happened here. Take a look at the graph; the price smashed through 2.40. It then came back down and tested that price twice. So in this case, 2.40 looks like the new floor. It then rises up to 2.50 and drops back down. It's quite possible that 2.50 will become the new ceiling but I'll wait until it is tested once or twice more before I try to trade that selection again.

EXAMPLE TWO

Figure 7.4 shows the Betfair graph for a selection which is currently trading at 5.20:

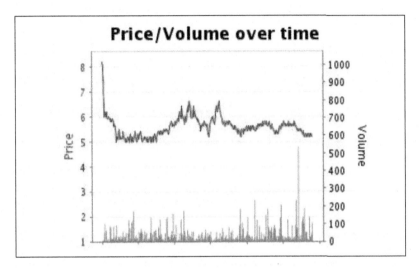

Figure 7.4

The ceiling price isn't quite so clear cut for this selection but the floor price is obviously around the 5.0 area. In the early trading, this price was tested numerous times before the price drifted back out. It came down close to 5.0 again a couple of times later on but didn't quite reach it — but I'd be fairly confident of a bounce if it does drop back down. The ceiling price is possibly around the 6.6 area but it hasn't really been tested all that much so in this case, I'd only try to trade the floor price instead.

EXAMPLE THREE

Figure 7.5 shows the graph of a selection that should be avoided.

Figure 7.5

There is no clear ceiling or floor here and the price is swinging in both directions in a rather erratic fashion. Remember; when trading support and resistance points, the floor or ceiling must be immediately obvious to the naked eye. Otherwise, stay away.

While I'm of the opinion that the markets are very often random, certain crowd behaviours can be found which prove useful to traders. If this were financial trading, I guess it would be called a technical analysis strategy (which is a fancy name for using charts) but I'm not too keen to pigeon-hole it into that category. Most chartists will try to predict which way the price will go based on the past but that's not what we are about here. Rather, we are trying to guess how the crowd will react to the chart and then react ourselves accordingly. There's an important difference between trying to predict the way the price will act, and trying to predict how the crowd will act. It's almost like a game of chess where you are thinking a couple of steps ahead. As you will have gathered by now, you don't have to try to predict which way the price will go to become a good trader and this is another 'sit and wait' strategy which allows you to take positions on both sides of the book. The key here though, is to have tight stop-losses in case of a breakout. Generally speaking, I'll try to earn one or two ticks profit with this strategy and will put my stop-loss two ticks below/above the floor/ceiling. In other words, the risk/reward ratio is 1:1. In the past, I used to use a strict one tick stop-loss but I found that I was getting taken out and losing quite a bit with what I call 'false breakouts'. This is where the price momentarily breaks through the floor or ceiling but then comes right back. It's extremely frustrating when you get stopped out on a false breakout so I've found that a two tick stop-loss generally helps avoid this situation. While ceilings and floors can be strong, they are not always made of glass and don't always shatter when broken. Think of them as being made out of cardboard — sometimes someone may punch a hole in them or bend them but overall, the cardboard remains in place. If a false breakout occurs and your stop is just one tick below the ceiling or floor, you may get hit for a loss. So if you are taking two ticks profit on your successful trades and taking a two tick loss on your losing ones, it's really a case of trying to get your strike rate above 50% in order to make money over time. It can take a while to get used to this so don't be too disheartened if you find that your strike rate starting out isn't quite 50% or higher. Keep at it, even if it's only with a pound or two. There's no substitute for experience and the more you trade, the more of a gut feel you will get for judging whether or not a support/resistance line is likely to prove strong. Take note too of the volume of money being traded. If the support and resistance lines are holding up well under strong volume, that's a good sign.

HIGH AND LOW

Something else worth noting is the absolute highest price and the absolute lowest price a selection has been matched at in the past. Note that these prices may not be the same as the current floor or ceiling. In the first example, the floor and ceiling were 2.30 and 2.40 respectively at the time we checked the market. But that was only during a twenty minute time frame. It's entirely possible that the selection had been matched at higher and lower prices in the past so check the graph to see if this is the case. If, for example, you find that the price was matched at a low of 2.20 earlier on that day, take note as this could be another 'bounce price' later on if the selection ends up trading back down at that level. It's sometimes difficult for a price to break out of its old barriers and make new ground and the highest and lowest prices matched in the past can often become extra ceilings and floors to bounce off. The funny thing is, the more people become aware of these bounce prices, the stronger the support and resistance they will offer. Indeed, it almost becomes a self-fulfilling prophecy as people will put in orders (building up a wall off money), expecting the bounce. The key here is to get in a little early so your money is near the top of the queue.

THE ANCHOR EFFECT

Readers who are interested in psychology may have heard of the 'anchor' effect. The anchor effect is what is known as a *cognitive bias* and relates to how the mind tends to rely on (often to our detriment) a certain piece of information which has been 'anchored' in the brain. This is particularly evident when it comes to shopping. When we go out to buy a product, we like to believe we are making a rational decision based on what we think is good value. But the truth is, we have no idea how much most things for sale are actually worth and rely on both the shops and other consumers to shape our ideas. The anchor effect has been used for decades in shops to good effect with so-called 'sale' items. Let's say you are browsing for a new pair of shoes and are thinking of spending about £50. You see a very nice pair of shoes with a 'for sale' tag attached to them. The old price was £140 but they are now marked down to £60. A bargain, that's £80 off! You then justify going over budget and spending £60 on a pair of shoes as you don't want to miss a great deal. This happens all the time. But how can we be certain we got a deal? Were the shoes really worth £140? Probably not. But the £140 anchor was set in your mind and you couldn't bear to miss out on 'saving' eighty quid. The true value of the shoes may have been something similar to all the other pairs which are on sale for £60 but you are not interested in all the other pairs as you had no anchor price for them. You've no concept of how much they are worth as you have no comparison price. The only reason you think £60 is a bargain for your particular pair of shoes is because the anchor price of £140 had been lodged in your brain. The price of £140 was probably unrealistic and the shop would never have sold them at £140 — but you still walk away somehow thinking you got a great bargain. I'll get to how this relates to prices when trading in a moment but for now, just be aware of the anchor effect concept.

BEEF IT UP

Another example can be seen when you go to a fast food restaurant; they will have the medium-sized meal only slightly cheaper than the large meal. Let's get something straight: the fast food joint may offer you lots of choices, but they really want you to buy the most expensive meal (which is the large one). Again, you have no real idea of how much it costs to source and make the food, how much the people serving it to you are getting paid, how much the rent on the building costs etc. so you can't really make a reliable call on how much the meal should cost. The human brain though, dislikes uncertainty and will scan for ideas as soon as you enter the building.

How do they get you to buy the large meal? They simply use an anchor. You look up at the menu board and see that a medium-sized meal is £6.40. This is the anchor. You then notice that the large meal is 'only' £6.90. Without you realising, your brain quickly works out that for an extra 50p, you will get a bigger meal. 50p for lots of extra food? A bargain! Only it's not. The medium meal was greatly overpriced — but that doesn't matter as the fast food place never wanted you to buy it anyway. It was simply an anchor for comparison which led you to believe the large meal was good value. The fast food outlet has done its job: it's sold you the dearest meal available but also convinced you that you got a good deal.

When it comes to betting and trading, the same anchoring principles apply and you need to be aware of them as they can help create resistance points. After all, backing or laying is no different than buying any other service. When you back or lay, you simply buy a bet. Generally speaking, most punters would not have the ability to price up an event from scratch. They need anchors. I've compiled odds for horseracing events and it's quite difficult to do. I'd advise you to try it — take a look at a sporting event and try to come up with a list of prices yourself — then go and compare it to the market and see how close you were. It's a lot harder than it sounds. That's why most people take the easy way out and allow themselves to be influenced by others. If you look at a horse race in the newspaper, for example, it's extremely hard not to be influenced by the tissue prices at the bottom of the page. Many punters come to rely on these prices and these prices can become anchors in our heads. We all like to think we are independently minded but if a horse was priced at even money in a paper like the *Racing Post*, that can then become the benchmark price for thousands of punters across Britain and Ireland. If this happens, prices around even money may become major areas of support or resistance on the exchanges. If it drifts too high, people may think there is no value in laying it anymore so the price may drop back down near the even money anchor. If the price goes too low, people will stop backing it until it rises back up near the anchor.

People also like to follow the crowd — some psychologists reckon it's a survival thing (safety in numbers) but for whatever reason, anchor prices that people perceive as being value can become hard to break, especially if that price is re-confirmed when they visit their betting site or exchange. As traders, we are not too concerned with why people think a certain price is a good value back or lay but we certainly need to be aware of the anchoring effect and how it can create price bands in trading. For more on the anchor effect, check out an excellent book by Dan Ariely called *Predictably Irrational: The Hidden Forces that Shape Our Decisions*.

Getting back to breakouts: as a general rule, I've found that breakouts are more likely if the prices are trading in a tight range. If there's a big gap between the ceiling and floor, there is less chance of the price making new ground. I read a good analogy somewhere which said resistance points were like the feet of a boxer — when the feet are close together, he is less stable and it's easy to knock him over, but when the feet are wide apart, he is much steadier.

On a side note, it's worth mentioning that you will often see strong support and resistance at certain 'traditional' betting prices such as 5/4, 11/8, 6/4, 7/4 and so on. This is due to the presence of old style non-trading punters in the markets. Even though the betting exchanges offer a vast array of prices to back and lay at, British and Irish punters grew up with fractional odds and still like to deal at these prices, even though they are now using exchanges. It's slightly strange in this computer age but if you offered someone 7/2 about a selection, they might take it. But if you offered the same punter 71/20 about the same selection, they'd have to stop and think (even though it's a slightly bigger price). Even though the exchanges are quite a modern concept, old habits die hard and that's why 4.5 (7/2) is much more likely to become a key price rather than 71/20 (4.55). One other small point: make sure the floor or ceiling price you are trading is not a crossover point (discussed in chapter four) as crossover prices have their own dynamic and should be traded separately.

THE MAGNET EFFECT

Never mind what others do; do better than yourself, beat your own record from day to day, and you are a success — William J. H. Boetcker, one of the first American motivational speakers

I'VE mentioned elsewhere in this book how people like round numbers and this is true in both the financial trading world as well as in the sports trading world. I do quite a bit of gold trading and there's always talk of which price it will break next. A few years back, people wondered if it would hit $1,000 per ounce. Once it went past that, people wondered about $1,200, then $1,500 and other round-number figures. At the time of writing, the price of gold is falling and now people are asking if it will drop back to $1,000. The fact is, people are drawn to round numbers for various reasons including their simplicity.

As discussed in chapter seven, people still like to bet at 'traditional' prices and this has carried through to the betting exchanges. So if I see a horse priced at 8.2 for example, I'd be more inclined to put my money on it hitting 8.0 rather than it hitting 8.4. It probably doesn't make much logical sense from a financial point of view but round numbers seem more attractive to punters and it's something to be aware of. I often call this the 'magnet effect' and simply being aware of it can be helpful when you are trading. You need to imagine that a round number is like a magnet and that the current price is like a piece of metal. Stray pieces of metal (the current price) will be drawn to the nearest magnet (the round number).

To explain more, take a look at figure 8.0. The picture shows a horse trading at 1.52 but I've also added in notes along the side of the ladder to help explain what is going on:

In this case, imagine that there are two magnets, both of which are competing and trying to draw the price nearer. The 'top magnet' is at 1.60 while the 'bottom magnet' is at 1.50. There is a neutral zone in the middle (prices 1.56, 1.55 and 1.54) in which the magnetic pull cannot be felt. As long as the price is in the neutral zone, it is not affected by either magnet.

Here, the price has left the neutral zone and entered the 'downward

Label (left)		Price	Amount	Label (right)
		2.74	78	
		2.72	122	
		1.60	48	
		1.59	64	
Top		1.60	22	Top
Upward magnet		1.59	97	Upward magnet
Upward magnet		1.58	154	Upward magnet
Upward magnet		1.57	255	Upward magnet
Neutral zone		1.56	245	Neutral zone
Neutral zone		1.55	76	Neutral zone
Neutral zone		1.54	318	Neutral zone
Downward magnet		1.53	316	Downward magnet
Downward magnet		1.52	217	Downward magnet
Downward magnet	294	1.51		Downward magnet
Bottom	274	1.50		Bottom
	60	1.49		
	142	1.48		
	79	1.47		

Figure 8.0

magnet zone'. Now that it is in this zone, the bottom magnet at 1.50 will attempt to drag the price down. The trade here is to back the selection when it enters the downward magnet zone (around 1.53 or 1.52) and lay it when it touches the bottom magnet at 1.50.

Had the price been in the upward magnet zone instead, the trade would have been a lay first, with an exit point at the top magnet (1.60).

Of course, sometimes a price will enter an upward magnet or downward magnet zone and not actually get pulled all the way to the magnet. In that case, we try to exit at breakeven or failing that, take a loss. Think of it like fishing; sometimes you get a pull on your line but it's not always possible to reel every fish in. When it goes wrong, you have to cut your line off and try again.

At bigger prices, the magnets get closer to each other as there are fewer increments in between (see chapter four for more on price increments). In my experience, it's not really possible to use the magnet strategy at prices above 10.5 as the magnet prices are just too close together.

Figure 8.1 shows another example of a magnet trade, only this time the price is much higher. The amount of pips (price increments) between 8.0 and 9.0 is far less than in the earlier example of 1.50 to 1.60. In this case, the neutral zone only extends across two pips (8.60 and 8.40). The price has just entered the upward market zone at 8.80 so the trade here is to lay at that price and exit the trade by backing at 9.0.

		9.60	122	
		9.40	32	
		9.20	126	
Top		9.00	191	Top
Upward magnet		8.80	152	Upward magnet
Neutral zone	194	8.60		Neutral zone
Neutral zone	195	8.40		Neutral zone
Downward magnet	77	8.20		Downward magnet
Bottom	87	8.00		Bottom
	22	7.80		
	88	7.60		
	47	7.40		

Figure 8.1

Once again, the thing I like about this strategy is that you don't have to try to predict which way the market will go — you just let it do its thing. As with some other strategies outlined in this book, it's important to get in early ahead of the queue. With magnet trading, you already know where your exit points will be so when you see a price trading in a neutral zone, you can put in your exit orders at both the top and the bottom of the magnet **before you open your trade**. This ensures that you will be ahead of the queue when the time comes to exit. Remember, the price may only touch the magnet for a very short time before bouncing back off so you need to make sure it is your money that gets taken. If you are at the back of a large queue, you won't be able to exit the trade. Note too that this strategy should not be tried on the 'key prices' (see chapter four) as they have their own dynamic and should be traded using a different strategy.

Timing is everything here and you don't want to open your trade too early. If I see a price that looks like it's going to enter a magnet zone, I don't just open my trade immediately. Wait until you see some good pressure (weight of movement) on that side of the book to confirm the price is actually on the move (for more on weight of movement and book pressure, see chapter twelve). You should also wait until you see the last of the money getting eaten away in the neutral zone before you jump in. In figure 8.1 for example, I would have waited until I saw the money getting eaten away at 8.6. If my stake was £100, I would wait until there was roughly that amount left at 8.6 and then I'd quickly fire in my bet. Hopefully, my money would have helped take out the remaining money at 8.6 and thus encouraged the price to move to 8.80. This is very much a short term strategy and if the price is taking its time to hit the magnet, then it's time to get out at breakeven point or a loss if necessary. Of course, in a fast-moving market, all of this can be trickier than it sounds and it might take some practice before you make it pay. But like most good strategies, the idea behind it is straightforward and it simply tries to take advantage of some people's attraction to round numbers and 'traditional' prices.

SPREAD TRADING

Never depend on a single source of income — Warren Buffet

WHILE this book mainly focuses on betting exchange trading, I thought it would be useful to include a chapter on the increasingly popular business of spread betting trading — and I'd also like to describe one of my favourite financial trading strategies; the S&P gap trade. Later chapters return to betting exchange trading. This is a stand-alone chapter; feel free to skip it if you have no interest in financial spread trading.

I began my trading career on the sports markets but when I went to buy some books on the topic, I found that there were very little available, much to my surprise. To compensate, I read as much as I could about financial trading and found that, broadly speaking, the same principles applied when it came to making (and losing) money. Some of the strategies I'd learned on the betting exchanges could be used to good effect in the spread trading markets and vice versa. In fact, I get quite a few emails each month from sports traders looking to broaden their horizons and my blog now deals with both financial trading and sports trading. So for that reason, I've included this chapter for anyone interested in taking the step over to financials.

Until relatively recently, buying or selling on the financial markets was cumbersome and there was very little room for the average man or woman with a small bankroll to speculate. To buy some gold for example, you would have to contact a broker who would do the deal on your behalf (for a fee of course), and most brokers weren't interested unless you had at least a few thousand in your back pocket. The vast majority of investors don't actually want to take delivery of the physical product so with a commodity like gold, there was often 'storage' or other related charges involved. When the time came to sell, you'd again have to contact the broker who would arrange the deal.

Investing in this manner was fine for people that had reasonably large sums of money and wanted to hold on to their investments for a few weeks, months or even years; but those looking to do some short-term trades with a small sum of money were left with very few options.

But in the past decade, some spread betting companies have set up in the UK and Ireland which allow both large and small stakes traders to participate in the markets. The difference though, is that these spread betting companies are essentially bookmakers (in fact, they use a bookmaking licence to operate legally). So rather than actually owning the product or shares, you are simply betting on the price going up or down.

In the old days, buying shares in a company through a broker meant that you legally owned a piece of that particular company. But if you 'buy' a company with a spread trading firm, you are really just betting that the price will rise and you **don't actually own any real shares**. If you 'sell' you are simply betting that the price will fall.

Spread trading is not for everyone though, and you need to make yourself aware of the risks. Most importantly, you can lose more than your initial stake. People are now starting to get their head around how it works but early on, spread betting received some negative press, often from ill-informed journalists who had tried and failed to make some money. The early bad press was somewhat unfair as most of the writers of those articles came at it from a traditional betting background and clearly didn't understand the different risks. Like everything, you need to understand how it works and what liabilities you are taking on before you decide to commit any serious money.

I'm not going to recommend one spread trading firm over another and it's up to the reader to decide which one best suits their needs. Personally, I use two certain firms which both have offices in my home city and are easily accessible if I have any problems, but shop around to find a firm that best suits your requirements. Some firms have better trading platforms than others, while the minimum stakes will also differ between companies. Will you need to contact a helpdesk? Do you need a sophisticated trading platform? Are you happy that your funds are secure? What size is your bankroll? Depending on how serious you become about trading, you will have to weigh up the pros and cons of each and I'm not going to use these pages to recommend any particular firm. Just remember though, that the spread trading firm is essentially a bookie (and therefore looking to keep your money) so always read the small print and don't be lured into a company which offers a poor level of service because of a special offer or free bet.

When I was setting up some accounts, one or two spread trading firms I spoke to were actually quite aggressive in their manner, trying to get me to lodge money by a certain date to avail myself of certain offers. If that happens, politely tell them you are not interested and hang up the phone. There's also been some concerns about the integrity of spread trading firms recently after one high profile company went bust (they had been illegally trading with customer money) but generally speaking, my experience of spread trading firms has been good and I don't have any real complaints. That said, I wouldn't trust any betting firm with my life savings and I never have more than a few grand in my account at any given time. I include the traditional bookmakers and exchanges in that too. As with anything in this world, a bit of common sense should see you right.

I'd definitely open a dummy account first as it can take some time to get used to the different setups and when you do start trading for real, just use pennies starting off. Like trading on Betfair or Betdaq, mistakes can be costly and you can lose money pretty darned fast if you don't know what you are doing. Having said that, there's only so much you can learn from a dummy account so when you figure out how it all works, I'd advise you to increase your stakes so that it hurts (just a little) when you lose. Trading with a dummy account or in pennies is great for learning how the particular piece of software works but in my view, you can only learn a certain amount from that and you don't always act the same when real money is on the line.

I once turned a £1,000 dummy account into £20,000 in the space of one month and while that looks amazing on paper, I made some completely crazy and reckless trades during that month that I never would have done had I been using real money. When there is real money on the line, we have very strong emotions to deal with so once you figure out how it all works, I'd advise opening a live account with a small bankroll that you can afford to lose.

HOW IT WORKS

With a vast array of charts, graphs and jargon to absorb, spread trading can seem intimidating at first. But the general concept is quite simple really.

For illustration purposes, we'll exclude the commission (or spread) that the spread trading firm takes on each trade and just give a simple example.

Let's say that you are interested in commodities and decide that gold is worth buying as you feel the price will rise. You log in to your account and note that gold is trading at $1575.50 per ounce. With most spread firms, gold is traded in increments of ten cents so a move to $1576.00 would be considered a five tick price move. In this case, you decide you are willing to risk £10 per tick and you click to 'buy gold' at $1575.50.

Let's assume you were correct in your assumption that the price would rise and later that day, gold was trading at $1577.10. As mentioned, prices move in increments of ten cents so that equates to a 16 tick price move. Your stake was £10 so your profit would be £10 x 16 = £160.

Of course had you been wrong and the price of gold fell, you would lose £10 for every ten cents price move down. While ladder interfaces are not very common in financial trading, figure 9.0 shows how the above trade would have looked on a ladder. The column on the right shows a range of gold prices, and the column on the left shows your potential profit or loss should the price reach that point:

As you can see, once we bought gold at $1575.50 per ounce using a £10 stake, we would win or lose £10 for every ten cents price move. In this case we sold out and took our profit of £160 when the price hit $1577.10. But you can also see the downside — had the price dropped, we would have lost £10 for every ten cent price move.

It's not hugely different from trading on the exchanges but unlike Betfair or Betdaq, you are not charged commission on winnings — the spread companies make money in another way.

In real life, if the true price of gold at a given time was $1575.50, the spread company would not actually let you buy or sell it at that price. They would insert a spread between the buy and sell prices they offer, somewhere in the region of four pips (price ticks). This would mean that the price on offer for you to buy might be $1575.70, while the price on offer for someone looking to sell would be around $1575.30. So basically, the spread is the difference between the current buy price and the current sell price, and in this case the spread is four ticks. It's no different from when you go to buy foreign

	£170.00	$1,577.20
Sold at:	£160.00	$1,577.10
	£150.00	$1,577.00
	£140.00	$1,576.90
	£130.00	$1,576.80
	£120.00	$1,576.70
	£110.00	$1,576.60
	£100.00	$1,576.50
	£90.00	$1,576.40
	£80.00	$1,576.30
	£70.00	$1,576.20
	£60.00	$1,576.10
	£50.00	$1,576.00
	£40.00	$1,575.90
	£30.00	$1,575.80
	£20.00	$1,575.70
	£10.00	$1,575.60
Bought at:	£0.00	$1,575.50
	-£10.00	$1,575.40
	-£20.00	$1,575.30
	-£30.00	$1,575.20
	-£40.00	$1,575.10
	-£50.00	$1,575.00
	-£60.00	$1,574.90

Figure 9.0

currencies in the bank — you will see a gap between the 'buy' price and the 'sell' price. Spread firms make their money in the same way.

The tighter the spread between the two prices, the better the deal it is for the trader. This is another consideration when deciding what spread firm to trade with. Some offer tighter spreads on certain products. Heavily traded products usually have the tightest spreads as the companies try to attract your business.

THE S&P 500 GAP STRATEGY

This is one of my favourite financial trading strategies and I actually know a man who makes most of his living from doing it. Personally, I'd hate to put all my eggs in one basket like that as there are no guarantees that it will work in the future — but to date, I've made a decent few quid from the S&P gap trade so I thought it worth mentioning in this book.

The Standard and Poor's 500 Index (aka S&P 500) is really just an index of some of the top traded companies in the US, and tracks their combined value. At one time, the Dow Jones used to be considered a good guide to the health of the American economy but that only lists 30 companies. So today, most traders agree that the S&P 500 is a far better guide to the state of their nation. It's a market value weighted index so each stock's weight is proportionate to its market value.

In short, it's a large basket of 500 companies and the S&P 500's overall value is a guide as to how well or otherwise those companies are doing collectively. You can research the S&P 500 online but to trade this strategy, you only really need to know a few basics.

Spread betting firms offer a number of options when trading the S&P 500. There's the general market which is open during regular trading hours Monday to Friday (don't forget the time difference) but the market we will be using here is the S&P 500 FUTURES market as this is open 24 hours per day.

Generally speaking, there are three large groups of traders which make the markets move worldwide on a continual basis. When the US markets close, the **Asian** traders take over and trade away (while we are all tucked up in bed). Then around 8.30am, London wakes up and it's now the **Europeans** who drive the market for a few hours. By 11.30am (UK and Irish time), the **Americans** are once again hitting their desks and they then take over from the Europeans for the afternoon and evening.

The idea behind this strategy is that generally speaking, Americans are essentially buyers of stock. In Europe, we think nothing of short selling our own companies but that's not the American way and for an American to short sell Coca-Cola or one of the big car companies is almost seen as unpatriotic. There are, of course, plenty of exceptions to this rule but generally speaking, as a nation, they prefer to buy rather than sell. Anyone who has been over to visit the United States can't help but be impressed by their enthusiasm and positive 'can do' attitude and this attitude can often be seen in the financial markets. A lot of the big hedge funds, for example, still like to buy the big American companies and don't get involved in short selling at all. In my view, it's a form of misplaced patriotism and that's what we attempt to exploit here.

TAKING ADVANTAGE

This trade should be carried out as close to 11.30 a.m. (UK and Irish time) as possible but if I'm out and about for the day, I often put it on earlier. The trade itself is quite simple:

1. Open up your charts and note what price the S&P 500 closed at the previous evening. If using the 24-hour market, note where the price was when the markets would have closed in the US.

2. Around 11.30 a.m. (UK and Irish time), check what price the S&P 500 is trading at. Have the Asians or Europeans driven the price down in the overnight/early morning trading session? If so, we have an opportunity to trade. The 'gap' is the difference in price between last night's close and this morning's current price.

3. If there is a large enough downside gap, buy the S&P 500 and wait for the Americans to hit their desks. When they do, they will see that those pesky Asians and Europeans have pushed the price of their S&P 500 downward. The cheek! The Americans hate to see gaps in the market, so they usually drive the price back up to close the gap.

4. Once the Americans have driven the price back up to around last night's close, it's time for you to sell and take your profit.

POINTS TO NOTE

I don't have a very strict rule about the size of the gap I'm looking to trade but generally speaking, I'm looking to earn about 80pts from this trade.

Make sure you know what increments the market moves in as it may differ depending on the spread trading firm you use. The account I use trades the S&P 500 in ten cent moves so if the S&P 500 closed at 1390.00 for example, an 80pt drop would be 1382.00. Regarding the length of the trade, I like to get out of my position by 3.30 p.m. whether I'm in profit or not. By that stage, the serious market players have taken over and the markets are moving on news, rather than patriotism or strategy.

EXAMPLE

Figure 9.1 shows an actual trade I completed recently and I've highlighted the important points of note:

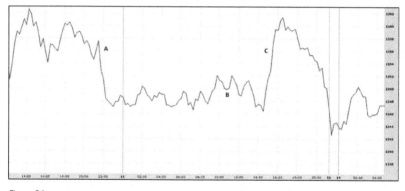

Figure 9.1

1. I opened this chart at 11 a.m. UK/Irish time and checked what price the S&P had been trading at the previous evening at 9.30 p.m. UK/Irish time (this is when the American markets close and the Asian traders take over). I've marked it above as point A. The price was 1357.60. As you can see, the price then dropped overnight in the Asian trade, and a 'gap' has been created.

2. The price at 11 a.m. (point B) is 1350.20. This is a downside gap of 74pts and while it's not quite the 80pts I normally look for, it's close enough so I open the trade by clicking the 'buy' button.

3. I wasn't around to watch the market that day so I put in an order to sell if or when the price hit my exit point. **My exit point is last night's close price** of 1357.60. As expected, the Americans drive the market up all afternoon and the gap is closed at about 3.30 p.m. (point C). This trade earns me £74 as I was trading £1 per ten cent price move. It's a nice few quid banked for very little work.

Spread trading the financial markets has allowed me to broaden my horizons and take some of my eggs out of the metaphorical sports trading basket. Plus, it gives me something to work on in the morning time when the sports markets are dead. Traders who have full-time jobs may find spread trading a refreshing alternative to the sports markets as most modern platforms offer easy automation. The particular strategy mentioned in this chapter is reasonably well-known in the financial trading world and as such, it is one of those trades that actually becomes a self-fulfilling prophecy. The more people that know the strategy, the more people buy the gap. As more people buy the gap, pressure is put on the price to rise. Quite often, you will see the prise rise sharply and then collapse back down as soon as the gap is closed so sometimes it is advisable to exit your trade a few points under last night's close. You may miss a few points profit by exiting early but you should catch most of the ride anyway. As the price approaches last night's close, the market often gets jittery. If I've already caught, say, three-quarters of the price move, I'll happily jump off and take my profit. One thing you will need to be aware of is news events. This is a strategy for quiet days where there's not much happening news-wise. Most of the main financial websites have sections which let you know what big announcements or events will be happening that day. If there's something big, such as non-farm payrolls or a major Federal Reserve announcement, stay away. Likewise if there's major news in Europe, this will have an effect on the market so to be on the safe side, just keep this one for the quiet non-news days. As regards stop losses, this is subjective. I don't mind taking a little bit of a risk on this as it has a high strike rate and I'll normally check the chart for major support and resistance areas and place my stops accordingly.

DUTCHING

Money is a terrible master but an excellent servant — 19th century
American businessman, scam artist and entertainer P.T. Barnum

FOUR guys are sitting in a pub, passing some time by watching horse racing on the TV. There's not a lot of luck about, except for one guy who seems to be backing the winner in nearly every race he dabbles in.

"Joe, what's your secret; how are you picking so many winners?" his friend asks.

"It's easy, I normally just stick a pin in the paper" replies Joe.

"But how come you've got it right nearly every time?" his friend wants to know.

"Well, today I decided to use a fork!"

OK, so comedy is not my strong point — but on that rather lame joke, we move on to the subject of Dutching. This isn't strictly trading, but it does differ from traditional backing and laying and most trading sofware packages now include a Dutching option. There's no real mystery to Dutching and it simply involves backing more than one selection in a race or event. But rather than using the same level stake on each selection, you work it out so that your return is the same, no matter which selections wins. For example, let's say you fancy two horses in a race, you have £50 to spend, and they are priced 3.5 and 4.5 respectively:

Most punters might throw a pony (£25) on each and hope for the best — but that would mean all is not equal:

- If the horse priced 3.5 won, the punter would collect £62.50 in profit for that bet, but lose £25 on the other horse, leaving a total profit of **£37.50**.
- If the horse priced 4.5 won, he would collect £87.50 in profit for that bet, but lose the £25 on the other horse, leaving a total profit of **£62.50**.

Of course, if both horses lose, the punter would lose £50. With Dutching, you want to win the same amount no matter which horse wins the race so instead of putting a pony on each, you would:

- Put £56.25 on the horse priced 3.5.
- Put £43.75 on the horse priced 4.5.

In this way, you would earn **£96.88** should the horse priced 3.5 win (£140.62 in profit, minus the £43.75 staked on the other horse). But similarly, you would also earn **£96.88** should the horse priced 4.5 win (£153.13 in profit, minus the £56.25 staked on the other horse). So with Dutching, there are only two possible outcomes: you win the set amount, or you lose the lot.

Thankfully, you don't need to do the sums yourself to work out the stake and a quick Google search of 'Dutching calculator' will bring up various options. Personally, I find the Oddschecker version very simple to use:

http://www.oddschecker.com/betting-tools/dutching-calculator.html

Of course, if you are using some trading software with a Dutching function, it should automatically work out the stakes for you and you should have the option of entering your total overall stake you wish to use, or else the overall profit you wish to achieve on the event.

A few years back, I read a book on betting which advised that you should never have a bet unless you have 100% faith in your selection. While I can see the point the author was trying to make, I think this is an outdated way of thinking. After all, doesn't the bookmaker have most of the field running for him in every race? There's nothing wrong with having more than one horse running for you — because things can, and do, go wrong all the time when we put our faith and our money into dumb four-legged animals. Or dumb two-legged humans for that matter. We've all been in situations where you back the 'good thing' in a horse race and it falls at the last fence. Wouldn't it be nice to have some insurance when that happens and have another one or two running for you? Yes, it can cost more money to Dutch but in certain limited circumstances, it is worth it.

Interestingly, Dutching all started long before the computer age and we can thank the United States legislators in the 1930s for giving rise to the practice when they ended prohibition. During the ban on alcohol, a gangster named Dutch Schultz, an associate of Al Capone, made a small fortune with his bootleg booze operation but it all came to an abrupt halt when the law changed and he had to think of new ways to make some money. Like a lot of us, 'Dutchy' saw gambling as an attractive way to make a quick buck so he started betting very large sums of money at the racetrack. At first, he was losing money hand over fist but after some time, his fortune changed and before long, he was winning money on practically every race. The details of his operation are unclear and I'm sure there's some lies thrown in somewhere but the story goes that he figured out a flaw in the odds machines — which were slow to react when large amounts of money went through them. When a lot of money was placed on a selection, it took a certain amount of time before the machine would drop the price. The net result of this flaw, it seems, was that he could get his team of helpers to back every selection in the race and still make a profit provided he timed it to perfection and used the correct stakes. He employed the services of a maths geek who was astonishingly fast with arithmetic and they made a tidy sum over the space of a few years.

As I say, I'm not entirely certain how accurate that story is but it does seem that Schultz certainly had some sort of system for backing more than one runner in each race — hence the term Dutching.

Which races and horses to pick is another story and is a matter for a different book, but generally speaking I like to focus on races where the favourite has a high probability of winning, then back it up with one or two others that follow in the market. In flat non-handicaps for example, the favourite has a strike rate of 49% in novice races, 41% in maiden races and 39% in Group One races (data is from 2003-2012). This compares favourably to the average strike rate of flat favourites (across all races) which is 32%.

So by sticking with these races, I know I have a fairly high chance of winning with the favourite alone, never mind the one or two others I add to the bet. Of course, backing any horses blindly won't produce a profit and I certainly wouldn't back in every one of those races — but with a bit of selectivity and some form study, it is possible to churn a small profit. It does require a bit of nerve though as most of the (overall) prices will be long odds-on.

But here's the interesting part — it is sometimes possible to Dutch every runner on Betfair and still make a profit by using some trading software. Not all vendors offer this facility but I know that Bet Angel has it as a feature. In chapter one, I mentioned the book percentages and the over-round. Most mature markets on Betfair will have an over-round of a couple of percent but on occasion, the book percentage will drop below 100%. When this happens, it is possible to make a guaranteed profit on the race by Dutching every runner. Conversely, when the book percentage goes above 100% on the lay side, it is possible to lay every runner and still make a profit. These opportunities rarely last more than a few seconds so it would be impossible to get the bets on without using software. On Bet Angel, you can select a specific Dutching function which will automatically fire the bets in with the appropriate stakes as soon as the book drops below 100%. All you have to do is simply enter your stake, turn on the function and wait. When the book drops, your bets are fired in automatically. Once the bet is complete, you then 'reload' your stakes and the software waits for another opportunity.

Figure 10.0 shows an example of a race from the 10th May 2013 at Downpatrick where the total SPs on Betfair add up to less than 100%. The book was settled at 98% (circled) which means it was under-round. So in theory, you could have backed every runner in this race and made a profit. By way of comparison, the industry SP over-round on this race was 126%.

On a rather glum side-note, I had a particular interest in this race as I had a share in *Vicky Miller*, the horse listed as pulled up. Sadly, she broke her leg coming down the hill which was a stark reminder that we are dealing with flesh and blood rather than simply numbers on a screen.

Of course with some markets moving quite fast, there will be occasions when the prices will have changed by the time your bet is actually fired in and some bets remain unmatched. In that case, you must decide whether to try get out at breakeven or sometimes it's necessary to accept a loss.

Be aware though, that Betfair have introduced 'cross matching' on a lot of their markets in recent times and this has seen quite a lot of opportunities dry up so it's harder to make money in this area than it was a few years back. Cross matching is quite technical and rather than explaining it all here, you should refer to Betfair's website to learn more about it.

Finally, let me issue a word of warning when it comes to Dutching: always read the market rules! There are certain markets where the book

FULL RESULT

Pos (Draw)	Dist	Horse	Age	Wgt (OR)	Eq	Jockey / Trainer	In-play High/Low	BSP/ISP (+/-)	Place
1		Shershewill	7	10-13	t	J. S. McGarvey (7) / Aaron Stronge, Ireland	6.4 / -	3.92 / 3.5 (11%)	1.63
2	1	Over Church Road	7	10-13	-	L. A. McKenna (7) / B. R. Hamilton, Ireland	- / 2.04	15 / 11 (33%)	4.2
3	2¼	Millie Le Bach	7	11-7	-	D. G. Lavery (5) / Thomas P. Cummins, Ireland	- / 3.15	5.4 / 5 (4%)	2.18
4	4¾	Cheyenne Girl	6	11-7	-	D. E. Splaine (5) / Patrick Martin, Ireland	- / 11.5	11.5 / 9 (25%)	3.15
5	2¾	Lol Jk	7	10-13	-	S. G. McDermott / Mrs Jeanette Riordan, Ireland	- / 10	16.76 / 17 (-6%)	4.75
6	7	Ultra Light	5	10-13	-	A. E. Lynch / Robert Hennessy, Ireland	- / 6	7.64 / 6 (26%)	2.54
7	3¼	Beaverstown Ash	6	10-13	-	Brian O'Connell / Mark Cahill, Ireland	- / 15	36.96 / 21 (71%)	8
8	1½	Dry Rain	8	10-13	-	A. P. Heskin / Benjamin Arthey, Ireland	- / 29	159.85 / 34 (357%)	32.74
9	½	Red Hot Milan	7	10-13	-	P. D. Kennedy (5) / Bernard Jones, Ireland	- / 70	77.4 / 26 (190%)	14
10	7	Country Class	6	10-13	-	M. J. Ferris / David Edward Finn, Ireland	- / 200	240 / 41 (468%)	80
11	36	Kings Fiddle	6	10-13	-	M. W. Bowes (5) / P. Fagan, Ireland	- / 10.5	60 / 26 (124%)	11
pu		Vicky Miller	5	10-13	-	Davy Condon / Gordon Elliott, Ireland	- / 2.84	7.78 / 6 (29%)	2.46

12 Ran, Winning Time: 4m 51.80s
Betfair SP Overround/Underround: 98%

Figure 10.0

percentage will be below 100% for a reason. It may look like a risk-free opportunity but there are very few free lunches in this world. I remember one occasion a few years back, I stumbled upon an Internet forum where a number of posters thought they'd struck gold. I can't quite remember if it was an X Factor market or a Big Brother market but it was one of those reality TV shows for which Betfair had set up a winner market. The people posting on the forum were all Dutching the winner market over and over yet the book percentage remained below 100%. How could this be? They all had fantastic green books and must have thought all their Christmases had come together. But reading the thread on the forum was like watching a car crash in slow motion and someone finally realised that the TV show would be adding extra participants to the programme each week. In other words, the market that they had been Dutching on Betfair was incomplete and as soon as Betfair added the new names to the show's winner market, all those beautiful green books turned a horrible shade of red.

Always be sure that the market you are Dutching is not a market where extra participants may be added as this will destroy your bet and put you into the red. It just goes to prove the old adage that if something looks too good to be true, it probably is.

ARBITRAGE

I don't throw darts at a board. I bet on sure things. Read Sun Tzu, The Art of War. *Every battle is won before it is ever fought* — Fictional 'Wall Street' movie anti-hero, Gordon Gekko

WHILE most of us love the idea of the betting exchanges, it's a sad fact of life that the rise of one entity usually involves the demise of another. Since the early part of this century, the art (and it is an art) of making a book has all but died out in the UK and Ireland, no more so than in the horseracing industry. The death of proper old-fashioned odds compiling and bookmaking in horseracing has been swift and the whole scene has changed so much since one spring day back in the year 2000 when I brought my girlfriend Krista (now wife) up to Leopardstown to let her experience a day at the races. Back then, a good proportion of the on-course bookmakers still used the old chalkboards rather than those characterless electronic boards and while the mobile phone had, by then, put the tic-tac men out of a job, each layer still had young 'runners' going back and forth for them, checking their rivals' prices, placing bets and reducing risk. With hardly a laptop in sight, the men that stood on boxes back then were tough, had plenty of nerve and would take a decent-sized bet without blinking an eye. Herself being from Canada (where making a book is largely illegal), she was fascinated by the hustle and bustle, the shouts of 'six to four the field' and the various wads of cash exchanging hands in a pre-recession Ireland that was brimming with confidence. I remember explaining the whole concept of making a book to her and although it was a little confusing at first, she loved the betting ring. The battles of wits going on in this little piece of turf in Dublin were as exciting as any you might see on the trading floors on Wall Street.

Roll on fourteen years and the scene in the betting ring at our local track on a recent visit was a far cry from those we witnessed back when we were, as the older folk would say, still courting. Take a walk through any betting ring in the UK or Ireland these days and you'd be hard-pressed to see a bit of competition on the now universal electronic boards and every single bookmaker will be taking his lead from what is happening on the exchanges.

Gone are most of the old bookie characters that would take a large bet and gone too are the legendary punters that took them on. The atmosphere is a lot quieter and with the recession, there is not as much cash floating about in these isles. I never thought I'd say it about the 'old enemy' but I actually feel sorry for some on-course bookmakers and I know one or two personally that struggle to make a living.

Some veteran bookmakers in the ring blame Betfair for their demise and although they have a point, the electronic age would surely have seen the industry change regardless of whether Andrew Black and Edward Wray had launched their new website in June of the millennium year. From a punting point of view, the books are now tighter and the odds are definitely better but the fact that any Tom Dick or Harry can now lay on the exchanges means that bookmakers won't offer higher prices as they will be taken advantage of by the arbers (Arbitrage).

While I miss the old days in the betting rings of Ireland and Britain I don't want to lament them too much and to quote William Shakespeare, "Cease to lament for that thou canst not help; and study help for that which thou lamentest". As mentioned earlier, some of the over-rounds on the books were terrible and it was difficult for any punter to make some cash. Now, we have quite a few angles to make money including what is known as arbitrage (or 'arbing' for short).

ARBING

In the mid 2000s, a good friend of mine used to make a living from arbitrage but in recent years, he feels that many opportunities have dried up and arbing has now become just a small sideline for him. Arbing basically involves making a profit from the difference in price that two separate bookmakers or exchanges are offering on a selection. In the early exchange days, arbing opportunities presented themselves daily but like any scheme that offers free money, it quickly became the talk of the town and too many market participants destroyed the gravy train. Occasionally, you still see the odd arbing opportunity but be warned; those who become known as arbers in the betting world are disliked by the bookmakers and if you do it for long enough, some will close your account.

EXAMPLE

On Thursday, 23rd August 2012, I opened up www.Oddschecker.com to check the prices for the Darley Yorkshire Oaks. This is a high-quality Group One race so there's a good chance that bookmakers will offer competitive prices as they compete for your business. Oddschecker is an odds comparison site and I rarely place a serious 'traditional' bet before visiting it. Simply select the event you want and Oddschecker will give you a list of bookmakers & exchanges where you can compare prices (figure 11.0):

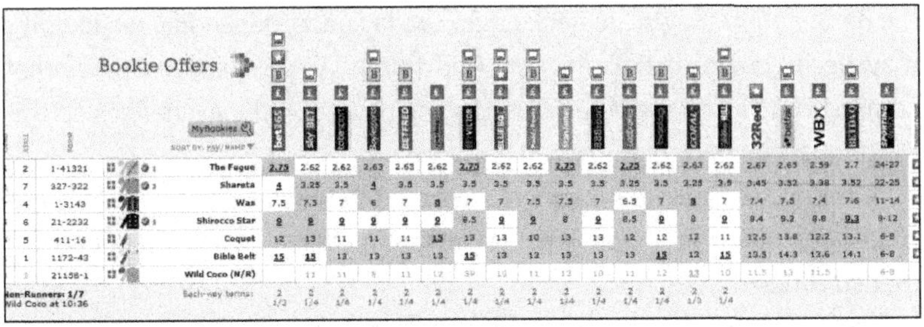

Bookie Offers
MyBookies
SORT BY: FAV/NAME

			bet365	sky BET	totesport	Boylesports	BETFRED		VICTOR							CORAL		32Red	betfair	WBX		SPORTING
2	1-41321	The Fugue	2.75	2.62	2.62	2.63	2.63	2.62	2.75	2.62	2.62	2.75	2.62	2.75	2.62	2.63	2.62	2.67	2.65	2.59	2.7	24-27
7	327-322	Shareta	4	3.25	3.5	4	3.5	3.5	3.5	3.5	3.5	3.5	3.5	3.25	3.5	3.25	3.5	3.45	3.52	3.38	3.52	22-25
4	1-3143	Was	7.5	7.5	7	6	7	8	7	7	7.5	7.5	7	6.5	7	8	7	7.4	7.5	7.4	7.6	11-14
6	21-2232	Shirocco Star	9	9	9	9	9	9	8.5	9	9	8	9	8.5	9	8	9	8.4	9.2	8.8	9.3	8-12
5	411-16	Coquet	12	13	11	11	11	15	13	13	10	13	13	12	12	12	11	12.5	13.8	12.2	13.1	6-8
1	1172-43	Bible Belt	15	15	13	13	13	13	15	13	12	13	13	13	15	13	15	13.5	14.3	13.6	14.1	6-8
3	21158-1	Wild Coco (N/R)		11	11	8	11	12	SP	10	11	12	10	11	12	13	10	11.5	13	11.5		6-8
Non-Runners: 1/7 Wild Coco at 10:36		Each-way terms:	2 1/2	2 1/4	2 1/4	2 1/4	2 1/4	2 1/4	2 1/4	2 1/4	2 1/4	2 1/4	2 1/4	2 1/4	2 1/4	2 1/3	2 1/4					

Figure 11.0

In this case, note that the French raider Shareta is available at 4.0 with both Bet365 and Boylesports (figure 11.1):

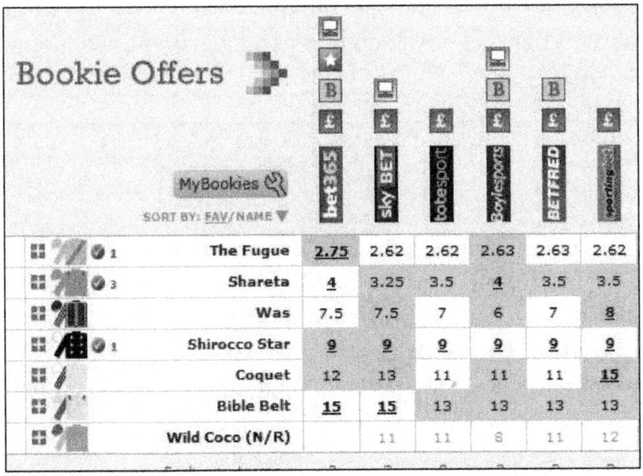

Bookie Offers
MyBookies
SORT BY: FAV/NAME

	bet365	sky BET	totesport	Boylesports	BETFRED	sportingbet
The Fugue	2.75	2.62	2.62	2.63	2.63	2.62
Shareta	4	3.25	3.5	4	3.5	3.5
Was	7.5	7.5	7	6	7	8
Shirocco Star	9	9	9	9	9	9
Coquet	12	13	11	11	11	15
Bible Belt	15	15	13	13	13	13
Wild Coco (N/R)		11	11	8	11	12

Figure 11.1

At the same time, Oddschecker tells me that *Shareta* is trading at 3.52 on Betfair and Betdaq and 3.38 on WBX. Unfortunately, I had recently withdrawn quite a bit of money from my Betdaq and WBX accounts to pay for a short holiday, meaning I only had Betfair to use for arbing. I potentially missed out on some free money here and it drives home the point that you should always keep your betting accounts topped up and ready for use.

At this stage, there are a couple of points to note. Firstly, there is often a slight time delay on Oddschecker so the odds displayed may have changed by the time you log into your Betfair and bookmaker accounts. Secondly, the Betfair odds shown are back odds. The lay odds, depending on liquidity, may be a couple of ticks higher. And thirdly, you must remember that commission will be deducted from a winning bet on the exchanges so this must be accounted for in the price.

I have over a dozen betting accounts in both Euro and Sterling — in this case, I use Euros as my Boylesports account, which was well funded, is in that currency.

Time is of the essence when you spot an opportunity like this so as quickly as I could, I logged into my Boylesports account to check that the 4.0 was still available. I got my betslip ready with the Boylesports account and in another screen, I opened up Betfair to check that the lay price was still considerably lower than 4.0. As you can see in figure 11.2, the price has since risen to 3.65 but this is still quite a good gap and a wonderful opportunity for an arb:

6 (2) The Fugue William Buick	2.7 €1983	2.72 €2917	2.74 €2752	2.76 €2772	2.78 €6842	2.8 €5187
2 (7) Shareta C. P. Lemaire	3.5 €3410	3.55 €2743	3.6 €1995	3.65 €827	3.7 €1362	3.75 €872
7 (4) Was Seamie Heffernan	7.4 €149	7.6 €323	7.8 €1621	8 €53	8.2 €590	8.4 €341
5 (6) Shirocco Star Richard Hughes	9 €1323	9.2 €546	9.4 €38	9.6 €105	9.8 €428	10 €543

Figure 11.2

As you can see, the Betfair market was very liquid with €827 available to lay at 3.65 so there was no problem getting my bet on. To make the arb, I simply:

- Backed *Shareta* at 4.0 on Boylesports
- Layed *Shareta* on Betfair at 3.65

It's really as basic as that. The money you make depends on the commission rate you have on Betfair. Let's assume that you are on the maximum commission of 5% on Betfair and you had both accounts well funded so they could handle a £500 bet. You would simply:

- Back the filly at 4.0 with £500 on Boylesports
  Lay the filly on Betfair with £555.56 (a liability of £1,472.22)

- If the filly wins, you earn £1,500 for the back bet on Boylesports but lose £1,472.22 for the lay bet on Betfair. **Total profit if *Shareta* wins: £27.78**.

- If the filly loses, you earn £527.79 (after 5% commission) for the lay on Betfair but lose the £500 from the back bet with Boylesports. **Total profit if *Shareta* loses: £27.79.**

So as you can see, you will be earning almost £28 no matter what the outcome. It's essential that you complete the arb as quickly as possible as the odds will no doubt change and the market will adjust and close the opportunity quite quickly. Thankfully, Oddschecker have a handy calculator on their site which quickly calculates how much you need to lay with to guarantee yourself some profit:

http://www.Oddschecker.com/betting-tools/hedging-calculator.html

Perhaps I'm not looking in the right markets, but I've noticed a sharp decline in arbing opportunities over the past few years so examples such as the above are always nice when they come along. Unlike the old days, I now find that the big events offer the best opportunities. Fair enough, £28 is not a huge amount of money but even if you got one or two a month, it may pay for your broadband or some other trading expense. On the downside, you need a large number of bookmaker accounts with money lodged in each to become a successful arber but this can tie up a lot of capital — although most bookmakers offer some sort of free bet when you sign up so that may offer a one-off opportunity in itself. Always look out for opportunities for arbing around the big racing festivals such as Cheltenham. People give out about bookmakers a lot and I do too, but I have to say that some of

Figure 11.3

the 'loss-leading' offers they had for Cheltenham in 2013 were outstanding. Some of the back offers were so good on their own it actually seemed a shame to lay them off! Take for example Coral's offer (figure 11.3) of even money on *Sprinter Sacre* to win the Queen Mother Champion Chase.

Fair enough, the maximum stake was only twenty quid but this was as close to buying money as one could get as *Sprinter Sacre* is a hugely talented horse. Those that wanted to double their money got a great deal but it was also a perfect arbing opportunity as *Sprinter Sacre* went off at 1.26 on Betfair as you can see in figure 11.4.

Had you fancied *Sprinter Sacre* to win, you could have backed him with twenty quid with Corals and layed him with twenty quid on Betfair. In that way, your liability on the horse on Betfair would be £5.20. Put simply, you cannot lose money. If the horse wins you earn twenty with Coral but lose £5.20 on Betfair so your total profit is £14.80. If the horse loses, you earn twenty (excluding commission) on Betfair but lose as much with Coral.

Of course the horse won in blinding fashion but there was also the option of making money either way. Had you put £20 on at evens with Coral and layed him with £33.06 on Betfair at 1.26, you would guarantee yourself £11.40 (assuming commission was 5%) no matter what the outcome. Again, you can use the online calculator to work out the stakes. People say

Sportingbet Queen Mother Champion Chase (Grade 1) (1)

Going: GOOD to SOFT (Old Course) | Distance: 2m | Age: 5yo+ | Total prize money: £365760 | Runners: 7 | Race Type: Chase

FULL RESULT

Pos (Draw)	Dist	Horse	Age	Wgt (OR)	Eq	Jockey Trainer	In-play High/Low	BSP/ISP (+/-)	Place
1 .		Sprinter Sacre	7	11-10	-	Barry Geraghty Nicky Henderson	1.28 / -	1.26 / 1.25 (-1%)	1.2
2 .	19	Sizing Europe	11	11-10	-	A. E. Lynch Henry de Bromhead, Ireland	- / 5.9	9.53 / 7 (35%)	1.97
3 .	6	Wishfull Thinking	10	11-10	t	Richard Johnson Philip Hobbs	- / 32	55 / 26 (105%)	5.14
4 .	3	Sanctuaire	7	11-10	-	R. Walsh Paul Nicholls	- / 25	29.04 / 21 (33%)	6.8
5 .	14	Tataniano	9	11-10	-	Andrew Thornton Richard Rowe	- / 380	449.1 / 101 (326%)	42
6 .	72	Mail De Bievre	8	11-10	-	Paddy Brennan Tom George	- / 24	30.53 / 21 (40%)	6.34
ur .		Somersby	9	11-10	cp	Dominic Elsworth Mick Channon	- / 50	58.54 / 34 (66%)	6.2

7 Ran, Winning Time: 3m 57.10s
Betfair SP Overround/Underround: 100%
Industry overround: 112%

Figure 11.4

there's no such thing as a free lunch but in this case, there was a free lunch on the table to the value of £11.40. Yes, it's not a huge amount but pennies make pounds over time. Here's yet another example in figure 11.5.

The picture shows some Ladbrokes special festival offers including Quevega to win the Mares' Hurdle at 2.0 (even money). As you can see in figure 11.6, Quevega won the race with a Betfair SP of 1.86.

It's not a huge gap but the maximum stake with Ladbrokes was a bit bigger at £50 so once again, there was free money on the table just waiting to be picked up.

THINGS TO NOTE ABOUT ARBING

There are some occupational hazards. Firstly, you may find that you get 'knocked back' by the bookmakers if you continue to do a lot of arbing. This means that they limit your bet size to a paltry amount or even close

▼ Cheltenham Festival - Best Price Favourites	
Non Runner No Bet Each Way Betting 4th place will be settled where applicable	
Selection	**Odds**
My Tent Or Yours - William Hill Supreme Novices' Hurdle	3.25
Simonsig - Racing Post Arkle	2.00
Our Mick - JLT Speciality Handicap Chase	9.00
Hurricane Fly - Stan James Champion Hurdle	3.50
Arabella Boy - Glenfarclas Handicap Chase	7.00
Quevega - OLBG Mares' Hurdle	2.00
Carlito Brigante - Rewards4Racing Novices' Chase	10.00
Back In Focus - John Oaksey Chase	8.00
Pont Alexandre - Neptune Novices' Hurdle	3.25
Boston Bob - RSA Chase	5.00
Sprinter Sacre- Queen Mother Champion Chase	1.40
Coral Cup - Edeymi	11.00
Saphir Du Rheu - Fred Winter Juvenile Hurdle	11.00

Figure 11.5

◀ **16:40** ▶ **Cheltenham**   ⬇ PDF Meeting Card

Olbg Mares' Hurdle (David Nicholson) (Grade 2) (1)
Going: Chase course: GOOD to SOFT (Old Course) Hurdles course: GOOD | Distance: 2m4f | Age: 4yo+ |
Total prize money: £85000 | Runners: 19 | Race Type: Hurdle

FULL RESULT

Pos (Draw)	Dist	Horse	Age	Wgt (OR)	Eq	Jockey Trainer	In-play High/Low	BSP/ISP (+/-)	Place
1 .		Quevega	9	11-5	-	R. Walsh W. P. Mullins, Ireland	5 / -	1.86 / 1.73 (12%)	1.21
2 .	1½	Sirene D'ainay	7	11-5	t	Jonathan Plouganou E. Clayeux, France	- / 2.1	54.63 / 34 (54%)	9.17
3 .	2	Swincombe Flame	7	11	t	Daryl Jacob Nick Williams	- / 7.8	50 / 41 (16%)	7.73
4 .	3	Shadow Eile	8	11-5	-	Andrew J. McNamara Mrs D. A. Love, Ireland	- / 2.02	210 / 67 (201%)	25
5 .	sh	Kauto Shiny	5	11-5	-	Paddy Brennan Tom George	- / 160	210 / 101 (99%)	19.5
6 .	1½	Prima Porta	7	11	-	Paul Moloney Evan Williams	- / 40	73.3 / 41 (72%)	13
7 .	½	Kentford Grey Lady	7	11	-	Noel Fehily Emma Lavelle	- / 2.52	14.64 / 13 (8%)	3
8 .	2	Shop Dj	8	11	t	A. P. Crowe Peter Fahey, Ireland	- / 46	49.47 / 34 (42%)	8.79

Figure 11.6

your account. Can you do without your bookie accounts? You have to weigh up the pros and cons before jumping in. You should also be sure to place the back bet first as some bookie markets have a maximum bet size. You don't want to lay the bet on the exchanges first only to find out later that you are knocked back or that you somehow can't back your way out of it with the bookmakers. Be sure too that the exchange market you plan on getting out with is liquid enough to absorb your bet easily. If you are taking advantage of a special deal, read the rules carefully. Can you withdraw the winnings immediately? Is all of your stake returned? Different offers will have different rules and it's easy to get caught out. Always check the rules of each particular market and remember that things like a Rule 4 deduction factor, when a horse is withdrawn from the race, may have a negative effect on your overall position. Over time, you must also ensure that you can move money from one account to another without much difficulty as one account will inevitably empty out while another fills up. Some bookmakers and exchanges charge money for certain types of withdrawals so if you don't have free bank transfers on your account, this too may eat away at your profit. As I say, there aren't too many arbing opportunities around on a normal racing day but even if you get one or two a month, you could clear a bill or two. Check the bookie Facebook and Twitter pages for special offers on the big Saturday races and also during the big festivals. Very often, they will offer out bets which are likely to cost them money. This may seem like bad business but once they have a punter on their hook, he is likely to continue to bet with them for the rest of the day or week, and he'll probably lose that money and then some more. So overall, it can actually make sense for the bookies to offer such 'losing' deals. As a trader/arber, you need to take advantage of the offer, earn your money, and then coldly pocket it and close down the screen. Don't keep on betting with it and don't be tempted to 'play up' your winnings. That's pure gambling. Once you've earned it, it's yours. Make sure you keep it.

WEIGHT OF MOVEMENT

Rodney: You mean you were gun-running in the middle of a civil war?
Grandad: Well that's the best time to do it Rodney, supply and demand!
(Only Fools and Horses)

I often hear people moan about the outrageous wages paid to footballers and other sports stars these days. With so much hunger and social deprivation in the world, it's a little disconcerting to see someone paid tens of thousands to kick a ball around a grassy field, but at the end of the day, it's a simple case of supply and demand and the football transfer market will ultimately decide what each player is worth. It may be obscene, but that's the system we have in place and until that system changes, there's no point in complaining. We are all familiar with the concept of supply and demand and we're surrounded by examples in our daily lives. From food shopping to airline flights, restaurants to petrol pumps; the more in demand a product or service is, the more it's going to cost the buyer. Of course, the same principles apply on the exchanges — if a lot of people want to back a selection, the price will become shorter (more expensive to back).

A horse or team etc. is said to be expensive to back if it would cost you a lot in stakes to win a fixed amount. For example, if you wanted to win £10 should your bet be successful, it would cost you £10 to back a horse at evens — but it would only cost you £1 to back a horse at 10/1. Therefore, the bet on the horse priced at evens is more expensive to buy than the bet on the horse priced at 10/1. And it's expensive for a reason — even money horses win a lot more than 10/1 shots.

These days, the prices in the sports markets are largely driven by the exchanges but to explain weight of movement in simple terms, (known as WOM) let's go back twenty years to the traditional on-course bookmaker pricing up a race.

The bookie would chalk up his prices around 20 minutes before the race and start touting for business. After some time, a clear favourite would emerge as punters put their money down on their fancies. If money kept arriving for a particular horse, the bookmaker would build up liabilities on that animal so he would have to take action to persuade punters to back other horses instead to even out his book (and avoid disaster should the fancied horse win). To do this, he would cut the price of the favourite and increase the price of the other horses. The increased prices on the other horses should prove attractive to punters and they may stop backing the favourite. If the bookmaker has a particularly large liability on a certain horse, he may send his helper around with some cash to actually back the favourite himself with another bookie, so he won't be too much out of pocket if the horse wins. This can cause a ripple effect as the bookmaker that just took the bet from the helper will now slash the price too. Sometimes, a cut in price would be enough to stem the flow of cash backing the horse but if punters were in the mood for a fight, they may keep on backing the horse, causing the bookmakers to cut the price even further. This is known as weight of movement in the industry: the sheer volume (or weight) of money arriving for the horse caused its price to move.

At the racetrack, you can't actually see how much money a bookmaker has taken for a particular horse but the beauty of the exchanges is that everything is transparent. Just like the old bookie example, if a lot of people want to back a horse on the exchanges, its price should get shorter and the price of another horse (or horses) should rise. Similarly, if a lot of people want to lay a horse on the exchanges, the price of it should drift. So to summarise WOM:

- If a lot of people want to BACK a selection, the price should fall
- If a lot of people want to LAY a selection, the price should rise

As mentioned, it's simple supply and demand stuff but because we can see the supply and demand for a selection on Betfair, it can help us with our trading decisions.

EXAMPLE

Take a look at figure 12.0 which shows the favourite's price from a recent race at Ayr.

		5.90	89
		5.80	555
		5.70	781
		5.60	1339
		5.50	1480
		5.40	3520
	8	5.30	
	187	5.20	
	41	5.10	
	209	5.00	
	77	4.80	
	1598	4.70	

Figure 12.0

This screenshot was taken roughly five minutes before the scheduled off time and while the current price is 5.40, the WOM for the horse on the back side suggests the horse's price should shorten. There is £3,520 looking to back the horse at 5.40, £1,480 at 5.50 and £1,339 at 5.60. But the layers opposing the horse are thin on the ground — there's almost no money at 5.30, there's just £187 at 5.20 and only £41 at 5.10. You can never be certain but all evidence points to a drop in price for this horse. How far it will drop in price remains to be seen but there's a clue at 4.70 with nearly £1,600 in the queue waiting to lay. Of course this could be a single trader trying to spoof the market and it's possible that they could pull their money out if the price approaches 4.70 but at the moment, we have no way of telling. People often put in large orders slightly away from the money with no intention of getting matched. Often, these spoofers are hoping to skew the WOM in a particular direction and get the ball rolling on a price move.

I didn't actually trade this horse as the price moved too quickly while I was trying to take the screenshot but in a case like this, I'd be happy to back the horse at 5.30 and 5.20 and then hope to lay out at 5.10. The reason I'd get out of the trade at 5.10 instead of 5.0 is because round numbers often prove difficult to break through (as discussed in chapter four) so I'd rather get in and out as quick as possible.

Just before the off, the price had dropped to 4.70 (figure 12.1) but the WOM is starting to build up on the lay side so this is where the price move runs out of steam:

	5.20	269	
	5.10	103	
	5.00	938	
	4.90	858	
	4.80	3497	
	4.70	2980	
3286	4.60		
1579	4.50		
1278	4.40		
878	4.30		

Figure 12.1

At this point, there is more liquidity in the market and you can see that the WOM is quite robust on both sides of the book, suggesting that the price may settle. The price bounced up and down slightly for a few more moments before the horse eventually went off at a Betfair SP of 4.80.

There's no great mystery to WOM and as mentioned earlier, it's basically just old-fashioned supply and demand. It's essential to know about WOM when trading but I'm not so sure one could make money purely 'following the money' these days. When I first began trading, it was possible to earn a few quid by simply watching how much money was in each queue but the markets are much more sophisticated these days and WOM has now become something I like to note, rather than using it on its own as a strategy. Bear in mind that in lightly traded markets, a single trader with a particularly large bank could put in false orders on one side of the book and make it look like the WOM is lopsided, so you must be particularly cautious when trading in minor events. That said, WOM can be a useful indicator of how the price might go, especially in busier markets (heavily traded markets are difficult for spoofers to manipulate) and combined with some other indicators or strategies, WOM should play an important role in your trading decisions.

There are other simple WOM indicators out there to help you find trades or at least give you an idea of how the market is shaping up. In this screenshot below (figure 12.2), I'm using the 'grid view' in the Betting Assistant software from Gruss:

		Selection name	Rev	Dutch	Price History	WOM		102.39%	98.54%				
12	Stubbs		□	□		2.5 €2785	4 €2531	4.1 €998	4.2 €1156	4.3 €616	4.4 €925	4.5 €369
11	Sir John Hawkins		□	□		9.2 €4949	6.4 €1671	6.6 €1757	6.8 €2123	7 €119	7.2 €299	7.4 €164
2	Championship		□	□		1.0 €38	7 €583	7.2 €372	7.4 €287	7.6 €493	7.8 €406	8 €481
14	Thunder Strike		□	□		1.1 €110	9.6 €156	9.8 €137	10 €997	10.5 €578	11 €607	11.5 €217
8	Riverboat Springs		□	□		2.0 €360	10 €223	10.5 €219	11 €281	11.5 €133	12 €102	12.5 €128

Figure 12.2

As you can see, the boxes on the back and lay side for each horse are displayed as normal in Betting Assistant but there's also a WOM box (circled) added in to give you extra information. Have a look at the horse named *Stubbs*; you will see a pink WOM box with the number 2.5 listed with €2,785 underneath. For now, I'll call the 2.5 the 'pressure figure'. These figures can help you decide how strong the book pressure is on a particular selection. In this case, the pink (lay) side is €2,785 stronger than the back side suggesting the price may rise. To get the figure of €2,785, Betting Assistant simply adds the numbers in the three back boxes together and the three lay boxes together and divides one into the other. So in this case:

2531 + 998 + 1156 = 4685

616 + 925 + 359 = 1900

4685 − 1900 = 2785

4685 divided by 1900 = 2.5 (pressure figure)

Here, the pressure to lay is 2.5 times stronger than the pressure to back. That's why the box is coloured pink. The horse below *Stubbs (Sir John Hawkins)* is quite interesting. There is €4,949 more waiting to lay than there is to back — with a very high lay pressure figure of 9.2. This strongly suggests the price of the horse is going to drift. Again, you have to watch out for spoofers or unusually large orders but this market was for Royal Ascot and was fairly robust a couple of hours before the races started.

At this point, it's worth taking a look at another key function. In figure 12.2, *Stubbs* is available to back at 4.2 and available to lay at 4.3. But if we take the price immediately available on offer, we could be doing ourselves out of a tick profit. I'm often surprised at how often people take the price presented to them, including traditional backers and layers. If you wanted to lay Stubbs, you could just settle for 4.3 but I'd sooner take a chance and put in an order at 4.2 instead. Most often, you'll get matched and it's always worth looking for that extra point.

In figure 12.3, I've clicked on the 'reverse book' function for Stubbs:

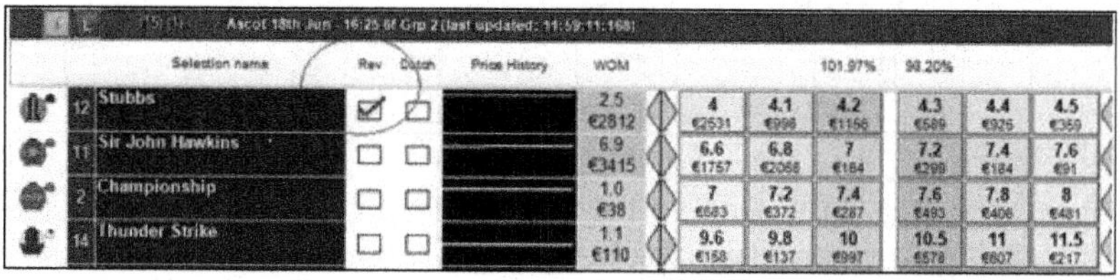

Figure 12.3

You can see now that if I want to lay, I can click pink at 4.2 and if I want to back, I can click blue at 4.3. This basically gives you the option of looking for the best price on both sides. Here, with two simple clicks, I could scalp the market by clicking on 4.2 and 4.3. This would put an order in on each side of the book rather than taking the best price available.

When trading, every tick is important and it's often worth the risk of not getting matched in an attempt to get a better price.

LAYING THE FIELD

Success is the child of audacity — Benjamin Disraeli

Down through the years, we've seen some amazing comebacks in sport and as such, there's been plenty of drama and carnage in Betfair's inplay markets. Who could forget Liverpool's remarkable comeback in the Champions League final of 2005? With AC Milan leading 3-0 at half-time, backers thought they were buying money on the Italian outfit and over 2.5 million pounds was matched at 1.01 before The Reds began their comeback in the 54th minute of the game and eventually won on penalties. Or when Arsenal were leading Newcastle 4-0 in 2011 and were trading at the floor price of 1.01? The Gunners later somehow lost a player and conceded four goals, and the match ended in a draw. In racing, I've seen quite a few 1.01 shots get beaten and I've also seen a handful of winners which were matched at the maximum price inplay of 1000.0. Sometimes I wonder if we'd see even more bizarre betting stories if Betfair allowed people to back/lay at higher/lower than 1.01 and 1000.0.

One strategy I enjoy in certain racing markets (although it can be done in other sports too) is laying the field (laying every horse) at an odds-on price and letting the bets go in-running. Of course, not all will get matched but depending on what price you lay at, you can get a payday every time a horse goes odds-on and gets beaten. This strategy is a work in progress and I'm still compiling my data so I'll keep it brief.

At one time, this was quite difficult to do as Betfair had no 'Keep In Play' button but we now have that option and it's extremely easy to do with some trading software. Take a look at Figure 13.0 below:

Figure 13.0

I've selected a horse race using Gruss Software's Betting Assistant and I'm going to lay the field in-running at 1.80. You can see that I've ticked the 'Keep In Play' box. I've entered a stake of €20, and in the 'Lay odds' box, I've put in 1.80. To lay the field, I simply click on the pink 'Lay field' button. It's as simple as that and each of my lay bets are now fired in at 1.80.

On the regular Betfair screen (figure 13.1), you can see how it looks. I've left an order to lay any horse for €20 if or when it hits 1.80 and my bets will be carried over when the event goes inplay:

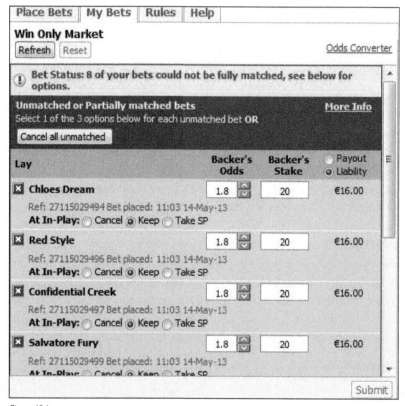

Figure 13.1

The worst case scenario here is that a horse travels better than the others throughout, wins the race, and no other runner hits 1.80 in-running. If that happens, I lose sixteen quid. But…

Suppose one horse appears to be going well and hits 1.80 in-running but then starts to struggle at the end of the race, allowing another horse to win. In that case, I win €20 for the first lay on the horse that appeared to be going well before losing — but I lose €16 on the horse that actually won the race. So in total, I earn €4 (excluding commission).

Actually, it's worth taking a look at the results of the above race as it turned out to be quite remarkable (2.10 Beverley, 14th May 2013):

- *Salvatore Fury* went off at 5.09 and traded at 1.22 in-running
- *Chloe's Dream* went off at 5.22 and traded at 1.27 in-running
- *Confidential Creek* went off at 3.25 and traded at 1.7 in-running
- The winner, *Auntie Mildred*, went off at 12.67 and traded at 900.0 in-running (figure 13.2)

◄ **14:10** ► **Beverley**   ⬇ PDF Meeting Card

Fantastic Prizes At Lucky In Love Selling Stakes (6)

Going: FIRM | Distance: 5f | Age: 3yo | Total prize money: £3500 | Runners: 8 | Race Type: Flat

FULL RESULT

Pos (Draw)	Dist	Horse	Age	Wgt (OR)	Eq	Jockey Trainer	In-play High/Low	BSP/ISP (+/-)	Place
1 (2)		Auntie Mildred	3	8-6	-	Silvestre De Sousa / David O'Meara	900 / -	12.67 / 11 (11%)	2.82
2 (1)	¾	Salvatore Fury	3	8-11	cp	Joe Fanning / Keith Dalgleish	- / 1.22	5.09 / 4 (29%)	1.74
3 (6)	½	Chloe's Dream	3	8-6	cp	P. J. McDonald / Ann Duffield	- / 1.27	5.22 / 4.33 (21%)	1.61
4 (7)	3	Confidential Creek	3	8-11	-	Frederik Tylicki / Ollie Pears	- / 1.7	3.25 / 3 (7%)	1.34
5 (4)	4½	Nors The Panic	3	8-11	e/s	Robbie Fitzpatrick / Richard Guest	- / 42	60 / 34 (70%)	6.66
6 (5)	¾	Twinwood Star	3	8-6	-	Raul Da Silva (3) / John Weymes	- / 22	42.81 / 26 (59%)	7.6
7 (8)	1¾	Red Style	3	8-11	b	Micky Fenton / Paul Midgley	- / 6	6 / 5 (19%)	1.9

7 Ran, Winning Time: 1m 3.08s
Betfair SP Overround/Underround: 98%
Industry overround: 117%
Non Runners: 7. Lady Calantha

Figure 13.2

This was a dream race for me and it must be pointed out that such rich pickings are quite rare but I won €60 from the successful lays (€20 each on Salvatore Fury, Chloe's Dream and Confidential Creek) and lost €16 on the winner, Auntie Mildred. That's a total win of €44 before commission. Not bad for a few minutes work, considering I could never have lost more than sixteen quid. It was one of those occasions where I wished I had used bigger stakes but as I say, it doesn't always work out so well and I'm still testing this strategy on different markets and collecting data.

The great thing about Gruss is that it allows you to use tiny stakes, pennies if you wish, when using this strategy. This is useful as it allows you to build up some data. This strategy works better on some markets than it does on others, and over time I hope to collect enough data to fine-tune it into a strategy that can be used on races that have a high likelihood of getting more than one horse matched in-running. As I say, I don't advise you do it blindly on every race (unless you are trying to build your data), selectively is the key here. Here are some things to consider when testing it out:

PRICES

I've used 1.8 in the example but who's to say that a shorter or longer price would not work better? Of course, if you go above 2.0, you will need more than two horses matched to make any money. Watch out too for large chunks of money in the queue at certain prices. If, for example, I see a large order at 1.80, I may lay at a tick higher to get ahead in the queue at 1.81 and sacrifice some profit. Note too, the SPs of the horses in the race. Does it work better with longer-priced favourites or short ones? Strong favourite or weak? Keep recording that data.

TIMING/NON-RUNNERS

This strategy can be done in the morning and left alone for the day but to be honest, you are better off placing your orders shortly before the race begins. A horse that is 1.90 in the morning for example, may well end up going off at 1.70 and if this happens, your order at 1.80 will have been taken already. You don't want to be laying horses at 1.80 that go off at 1.70 so it's best to wait until the off-time approaches. Similarly, non-runners will mess up your data as a reduction factor will be applied to your bets. When gathering data, we want consistency — but that can prove troublesome when horses get withdrawn from races.

RACECOURSES

I don't have enough data to tell whether this is purely random or not — but certain courses see significantly more horses get matched odds-on in-running and then lose the race. Know your courses well. Is there a long or short run-in which could catch punters out? Is it one of those tricky courses which can catch an inexperienced jockey out?

DISTANCE

Again, I don't have enough data to draw any meaningful conclusions but I've found that longer races have proved the most profitable so far, perhaps because a horse can appear to be going well for quite some time allowing punters to get their bets on. In a quick sprint, a horse may go well for a few seconds but it may not be long enough for punters to push the prices right down. That said, I'm working on some strategies in the sprints at certain courses which seems to be going well.

Remember too that trends change over time and what is profitable now may not be profitable in a few years. That's why it's important to keep recording data, even if it is with pennies. Make sure you have a meaningful amount of data before you hit it with big stakes. Overall though, it's a nice little strategy — it's simple enough, requires very little thought (other than when you sift through your data) and if using software, it only takes a second to get the bets on before each race.

MANAGING EXPECTATIONS

Compound interest is the eighth wonder of the world. He who understands it, earns it ... he who doesn't ... pays it — Albert Einstein

We'll come back to strategies shortly but I thought it would be useful at this point to talk about expectations. Over the years, I've helped a number of people learn how to trade in both the financial markets and on the betting exchanges and the one thing I've found common among all new students is a lack of perspective about how much they are going to earn (if they end up good enough to churn a profit). I'm going to say it now loud and clear: lower your expectations! I'm not saying you shouldn't reach for the stars and if that Tony Robbins audiobook gives you a lift every morning in the car, more power to you. But when it comes to trading, unrealistic expectations can completely destroy your trading career before it begins and I've seen so many people end up on the metaphorical scrapheap early on even though they have actually mastered the techniques needed to provide a second income from trading. Trading takes time. A lot of time. It takes months, years even, to build up a decent-sized bank. Far too many traders give up or become reckless when the life they've always dreamed of doesn't land on their lap after a few short weeks of trading. Knowing what to expect and being able to separate your dreams from reality should help you cope with a job which is essentially a very slow burner.

To get an idea of how realistic you are, let me ask you to imagine the following scenario...

Scenario one: You've saved up hard, you've done some trading courses, read some books and you finally feel ready to give trading a go. You've been making profit on paper, but it's time to use real money. You lodge your savings into Betfair and your balance is £1,000. After a busy first day where you made some good and some bad calls, the day's sporting action finally comes to an end. You check your profit and loss for the day. You are up £1.67 after eight hours of trading.

How would you feel? Would you be disappointed? Would you feel that you wasted your time? After eight hours, you are only up £1.67, which effectively means you were earning around 21p per hour on average. 21p per hour? This trading business might not seem so glamorous after all. But let me ask you to imagine another situation and see if you feel the same way...

Scenario two: You've been a trader for three years. You've had many winning days and many losing days but overall, your profits are building nicely. In fact, when you plot your profit and loss on a graph, it shows a steady curve upwards. You've stuck to your rules, never put too much capital at risk and you are finally earning some serious money. Your £1,000 starting bank now stands at £5,800, a 480% increase in three years.

Most people I've taught to trade have said they wouldn't feel any sense of achievement at earning £1.67 trading for a single day with a £1,000 bank. Yet the same people say they would feel absolutely fantastic at turning a £1,000 bank into £5,800 after three years. Why is this so? Both sets of results have something in common so we should be happy with both situations.

Going back to the first scenario, let's assume you continue to trade for a month and earn roughly £1.67 each day. At the end of the month, your bank would be approximately £1,050. In other words, you would have increased your bank by 5% in a month. Can you see where this is going?

Increasing your bank by 5% is a fantastic achievement so there is no need to feel bad about earning £1.67 for a day of trading. If you increased that bank of £1,050 by 5% the following month, the new total would be £1,102.50. Now we are getting somewhere.

Assuming you could increase your bank by 5% per month, the impact of compounding means the bank would be over £1,795 after twelve months of trading. Of course, it will never be as smooth as all that and there will be some good months and some bad months thrown in too — but overall, you get my point.

Increasing your bank by 5% per month would see your £1,000 increase by nearly 80% in a single year. The below is very simplified, but figure

Month	Bank	Add 5%	New bank
January	£1,000.00	£50.00	£1,050.00
February	£1,050.00	£52.50	£1,102.50
March	£1,102.50	£55.13	£1,157.63
April	£1,157.63	£57.88	£1,215.51
May	£1,215.51	£60.78	£1,276.28
June	£1,276.28	£63.81	£1,340.10
July	£1,340.10	£67.00	£1,407.10
August	£1,407.10	£70.36	£1,477.46
September	£1,477.46	£73.87	£1,551.33
October	£1,551.33	£77.57	£1,628.89
November	£1,628.89	£81.44	£1,710.34
December	£1,710.34	£85.52	£1,795.86

Figure 14.0

14.0 shows a chart tracking progress where you can see the power of compounding at work:

As you can see, the bank at the end of year one is nearly £1,800. If you continued in this vein and increased your bank by 5% each month for a second year, the bank would stand at £3,255.10. And finally, if you increased that £3,255.10 by 5% each month in year three, the bank would stand at £5,791.82.

Bingo! We began with scenario one but have now arrived at scenario two.

Hopefully by now, you can see both situations in a new light. I can fully understand how a return of a pound or two after a full day of trading can seem paltry, especially if you are stuck for a bit of cash and were hoping to generate a second income. But there are no shortcuts in this business and you have to be in for the long haul.

BEATING THE BEST IN THE WORLD?

As mentioned, earning a profit of 5% per month means you would be increasing your bank by around 80% per year and being honest, even this might be a little unrealistic for most traders. Many traders expect to double, treble or even quadruple their bank in the space of a few months but this is wildly optimistic. To put those sorts of returns into perspective, consider the *Berkshire Hathaway* fund, largely controlled by Warren Buffet who is widely regarded as one of the greatest financial traders/investors of all time. Over the last four decades, *Berkshire Hathaway* has grown by an average of 20% per year. This is considered a phenomenal achievement in the financial world.

That's what I'm saying about being realistic; the greatest trader/investor in the world manages returns of 20% per year. Keep that in mind when your bank is only up a couple of pounds in the beginning.

Generally speaking, if I can earn 3% per month, I'm very satisfied. Don't forget, 3% per month compounded will see your bank increase by over 40% in the space of a year. If you still somehow don't find that impressive, go down to your local bank and ask for 40% per year on your savings. And then wait while they call the men in white coats to take you away. If you have a long-term view, realistic expectations and understand that pennies make pounds, you can then concentrate on the business of increasing your bank each month rather than focusing on the individual daily returns early on.

EXPERT LOSERS

Let me tell you a quick story. Nearly a decade and a half ago, a pension advisor came around to my workplace to talk to us about the future. I was about twenty years of age, living in a flat I could hardly afford, and was basically broke. But the pension salesman, who was from a very reputable firm I might add, painted a picture of my retirement and what it would be like to have no money to fall back on later in life. The picture he painted wasn't nice and I fell hook, line and sinker for his sales pitch, which promised a small but useful retirement fund when I do reach sixty-five, provided I paid the insurance company £15 per week. The pension company, I was told, were experts in investment and would manage my deposits on my behalf. I scrimped and saved to pay the money each week but after a year or so, I just couldn't afford it following an increase in my rent so I had the bank cancel my payments. I figured that I needed the money more when I was young, rather than when I was old. Overall, I had paid about 800 quid into the scheme and that money is still under their control as I signed a form to say it wouldn't be given back to me until I retire. Here's the killer; the 'experts' that managed my money over all those years have, somehow, turned the 800 quid into the rather paltry sum of £200 today. Each year, they send me an account statement to let me know how they are doing with my money, and each year my money reduces even further. I just laugh at it now and thank the heavens I gave up paying into it when I did. Apparently, the 'blue chip' companies they invested my money in included banks. Now, if you are familiar with the banking system in Ireland, you will know that some bank shares are as useful as a chocolate teapot these days. It's the same in the UK and while I got out lightly losing a few hundred, so many people have seen their life savings wiped out by pension funds which mismanaged their money.

The point I'm making here is that so-called experts in money management have proved no better than you or I at managing money. So don't be afraid to take control of your situation and trade your own money. Would you be disappointed if your trading bank of £800 was reduced to £200 by making bad trades? Of course you would but that's exactly what happened to me when I left it to the "experts". I'm quite certain that if you handed me £800 in the morning, I'd manage to do a lot better than turn it into £200 over the space of a decade.

This all ties back to my original point about managing expectations. Compared to those experts that managed my pension fund, the trader who earned £1.67 for a day's work was doing fantastically well.

If you manage your expectations, accept that there will be PLENTY of losing days, set realistic targets, forget the Ferrari for now and be man (or woman) enough to take responsibility for your mistakes, then you can lose the fear and get on with building your bank.

STAKING

People often ask me about staking and what plan they should use but there is no simple answer because everyone's personality and circumstances are different. Some people are more risk averse than others but the goal of every trader should be to **protect their capital**. Respect your money and stay in the game. Yes, it's horrible to have a losing day and yes, it is very tempting to try to recover those losses just so you can avoid posting a red figure in the spreadsheet — but as I have learned the hard way down the years, you will only get away with loss chasing for so long and eventually, it will blow up in your face. Reckless trading, loss chasing and risking large portions of your bank on individual trades is not really trading. It's gambling, pure and simple. As humans, we like to compartmentalise our time and most of you will look at your trading results in terms of winning days or weeks — but this is a fallacy as the market is an ongoing entity that doesn't really have an end. I do admit that it feels much better to close down the computer after I've had a winning day rather than a losing one but in the grand scheme of things, your results for any given day are not all that important. If you are seeing very big wins or losses on individual days, it's a sure sign that you are staking too much money on each trade.

But looking at the bigger picture can be hard to do sometimes and some people just can't stop checking their profit and loss for the day. If you are finding it difficult to see the bigger picture, consider quitting trading for the day if a certain amount of money is lost. For example, if you were trading a £1,000 bank, you might decide to quit for the day if you lose £40. Simply close down the computer and walk away. When you are down money, it's almost impossible to resist the urge to get that money back and even if you hit a nice trade and earn, say £30 back, your day will still seem like an unsuccessful one. It's very difficult to keep a clear head if you have an urge to get back your losses and in all likelihood, it will lead to reckless trading which will further compound your losses. Your judgement is clouded and trading will become emotional. Trading while having various strong emotions is a big no-no. Walking away with a fifty quid loss is never nice but it's not half as depressing as digging yourself into a deeper hole with an unclear head. It's a much used phrase but 'there's always tomorrow'. When you start afresh the next day the slate is clean and you won't feel so much like you are fifty quid behind.

Personally, I've become quite risk averse in recent years and would rarely risk more than 3% of my bankroll on any given trade. How much I risk depends on what strategy I'm using and how successful that strategy is over time. If, for example, I'm using a strategy that has an average success rate of 20%, I would risk 2% of my bank on the trade. If the strategy had a success rate of 30%, I would risk 3% of the trade and so on. But I have an upper limit of 5% of the bank which must not be crossed under any circumstances. Mostly though, 1% to 2% of your bank should be the amount you risk on any given trade, especially if you are a beginner.

Using a percentage of the bank to risk on each trade is useful as, in theory anyway, your bank can never really go bust (although in a practical sense it can). And when the good times come, using a percentage of the bank will help compound your profit as the stakes are increased as the bank builds up.

The key point is that you must stay in the game. It's like a boxing match. You can have a bad round but still win the fight as long as you don't get knocked out. It's the same with trading — you can have bad days, weeks or even months but recovery is only possible if you protect your capital. While I do admit that it's easier said than done, your objective should be to trade well, rather than make a profit each day or week. If you concentrate on trading well, the rewards will follow naturally over time. While it might not seem like it, walking away from the computer when your daily loss limit is hit can be considered good trading. Sticking to your limits and only risking a percentage of the bank is also good trading, even if you show a loss for the day. Focusing solely on your chosen set-ups and strategies is considered good trading. The thing is, good traders have bad days. But over time, they reap the rewards for being good traders.

It's probably against the law to hire young teenagers these days but when I was fourteen, I got a job in a pub at night. Some nights, the bar would be practically empty and after paying the wages and bills for the night, the owner would have made a loss. But other nights, a crowd might come in from work, there might be a match on the TV, or someone would book a birthday party and we would be jam-packed. The till would be overflowing and the owner would have a big smile on his face. The rare good nights made up for the many bad nights, and overall the pub made money over time — even though there were plenty of 'losing' nights along the way when the bar would be empty. But the pub had to make sure it had enough money to open the doors seven days a week and pay the wages, as you never knew which night would turn out to be a success. Like any good businessman, the owner could see the long-term picture and didn't throw the toys out of the pram when he had a bad night with no customers. And make no mistake, trading is very much a business too, so treat your trading capital with the respect it deserves.

Focus on being a good trader, realise that being a good trader involves plenty of losing as well as winning, and eventually the money will look after itself. I'll repeat what I said earlier as it's something all good traders understand:

The most important thing in trading is to protect your capital and **stay in the game**.

TRADING INPLAY

It's not enough to succeed. Others must fail — Gore Vidal

I grew up in the 1980s so I don't consider myself all that old, but times do change quickly and the betting scene back then was a world apart from what it is now. I mentioned in an earlier chapter how quickly things have moved on since the turn of the century and if you are under the age of 25, there's a good chance you won't remember the old poky, smoky betting shops with a chalk board on the wall for the odds and one TV (if you were lucky) stuck in the corner. While never a huge gambler, my father did like a few bets and every Saturday he'd have a flick through the now defunct Sporting Life newspaper and pick out his horses. They didn't mind children being in bookies back then and off we'd go to the local shop where the same man would be sitting behind the counter taking the bets each week. I later learned that this man was the owner of the bookies, and he had bought himself a shop after spending a number of years laying bets on-course.

What's the point in this history lesson? Well, I just want to illustrate how it was much simpler back then, even though the over-rounds were very high. You had a bet with the bookie, and either you won or he did. Simple as that. While we never want to go back to those days, I do think some punters can become bedazzled by the modern plasma TVs, the 'free' coffee and tea and the flashing computer screens that populate bookie shops today. The person taking your bet behind the counter is most likely to be working for one of the big companies and doesn't really care if you win or lose as they will be getting paid anyway. Slick advertising and fresh bright shops make betting seem like a fun thing to do but I sometimes feel that people are losing sight of the fact that this is a zero-sum game. For every winner, there has to be a loser and there's no getting away from that. Most often, it's the punter that loses. In the old days, the bookmaker knew his customers by name and it really was a simple case of pitting your wits against another man. With such an array of betting markets and games today though, it's easy for the casual punter to lose track of how much he is winning and losing.

Speaking of being blinded by technology, it's the same with those of us who bet or trade from home. I've seen punters and traders spend thousands on the latest multi-screen set-ups, top-notch computers and all that goes with it. I'm not immune to this myself and at times my office at home looks like something from a London City trading room. All very impressive, and it makes me look like a big shot when I have visitors around — but it doesn't necessarily make me a better trader. A big ego can be dangerous in this game. I once heard about someone who sticks a £20 note on the wall next to his computer when he's trading to remind him that the numbers on the screen are real money and for every winner there has to be a loser (no matter how sophisticated their set-up is). In my home, I couldn't leave a score lying around or the missus would be off down to the shops in a flash! But the point I'm trying to make is that you should always remember that every time money flows out of your account, it ends up in someone else's. You can blame bad luck, bad jockeys, bad players, the market or anything else you like — but when you lose money, it's usually because you've been outwitted by someone else.

Like most traders, I have a secret admiration for the fictional 'Wall Street' anti-hero Gordon Gekko and if you haven't seen that movie, you should check it out as the one-liners are fantastic. In one scene, Gekko sums up trading well when he says:

'It's a zero-sum game; somebody wins, somebody loses. Money itself isn't lost or made; it's simply transferred from one perception to another.'

That brings me on to the topic of inplay trading (sometimes called in-running trading) and it's a subject I was originally going to exclude from this book as I'm certainly no expert. I have found a couple of edges in the inplay markets in recent times but they can't be explained in straightforward steps like some of the other strategies in this book so I thought it would be best to ignore the topic. But I later changed my mind and decided that I'd nothing to lose by discussing my inplay approach as long as I make it clear to the reader that I very much have the metaphorical 'L plates' on in this area. I should also note that I've only managed to make money on inplay on horseracing; I'll leave the inplay trading on other sports to better brains than mine.

A BRIEF INPLAY HISTORY

While definitely a modern concept, inplay trading sometimes reminds me of the aforementioned betting days of old, as there's less money available in the markets compared with the pre-race volumes and you can often get a real feeling for the other market participant(s) against whom you are pitting your wits. Indeed, it's sometimes possible to spot individual players in a quiet market who may, for example, be using similar-sized stakes on each race. There's a real buzz from betting inplay although the days of making a profit watching *At The Races* or *Racing UK* on your SKY box from home are long gone.

In the early days, a good deal of punters thought inplay trading would be a quick way to make some easy money but it soon became clear that certain TV pictures were faster than others and that a two or three second delay can make a world of difference, especially in jump racing where horses fall on a regular basis. I remember a few years back taking the old 'rabbit ears' out of the attic and sticking them on top of my TV in Ireland to pick up the Leopardstown Christmas Festival, which was broadcast on terrestrial TV by the National broadcaster RTÉ. I checked the coverage against At The Races on my SKY box on another TV and lo and behold, the old rabbit ears were broadcasting the pictures a full five seconds faster. The fact that no UK punters had access to the RTÉ pictures gave Irish terrestrial viewers an absolutely massive advantage. As far as I know, there was a similar situation in Britain where racing on terrestrial BBC, for example, was a good few seconds faster than SKY.

Soon, inplay 'trading rooms' began to spring up in London, Dublin and elsewhere and they quickly became the place to go as they could boast live TV feed from the racecourses and offer super-fast broadband. For a time, there was money to be made in these rooms but as mobile Internet became more advanced, people started bringing their laptops to the actual racecourse so they could bet in real-time on what they were seeing in front of them. All the high-tech fibre optic cables in the world can't compete with the naked eye and the trading rooms have shut down in recent years. Indeed, since the downturn in the economy (which saw racecourse attendances fall) some racing venues even started offering out the old corporate boxes for hire to inplay punters as a way to get customers through the turnstiles — which means that it's now next to impossible to make a profit sitting in front of a TV screen. The message here is simple: if you are still betting inplay using your TV screen at home, stop now as you simply can't compete. Those of us who used to use the trading rooms were left in limbo, certainly in Ireland anyway. I hadn't got the time to travel around to the racecourses every day and besides, most of the racecourses in Ireland are not exactly Wi-Fi hotspots. But I knew that there had to be some trading profit to be made from the wildly fluctuating inplay odds on horseracing and an idea came to me while watching one of my all-time favourite horses, Big Buck's, battling back to win the 2010 Liverpool Hurdle at Aintree. Best of all, the strategy doesn't require the use of TV pictures.

MAKING A BUCK FROM BIG BUCK'S

Anyone who knows their racing well will be aware that *Big Buck*'s would often hit a 'flat' spot midway through the race and get a little lazy. There are quite a few horses which do this. At times, he would even appear to be struggling but when push came to shove, he always had an extra couple of gears and he'd win his races comfortably in the end. Even though *Big Buck*'s would hit this flat spot most times he ran, his price would still rise in-running when it happened. I guess the people pushing his price out were those who were simply betting on what they were seeing in front of them, rather than those who knew the formbook inside out. With a small bit of research, there was some easy money to be made on the likes of *Big Buck*'s. All you'd have to do is lay him pre-race and then leave an order to back him at a higher price in anticipation of the price rise when he hit the usual flat spot and punters started to panic.

As some readers will know, trainer Paul Nicholls tried *Big Buck*'s out as a chaser but it didn't work out. He then reverted back to hurdles and the horse became one of the most successful staying hurdlers of all time. Figure 15.0 shows a list of his races since he returned to hurdling including his Betfair SP, and how high he traded inplay:

Date	Course	Betfair SP	Inplay high	Price rise?	Price rise %
01-Dec-12	Newbury	1.11	1.11	No	0.00
12-Apr-12	Aintree	1.25	1.25	No	0.00
15-Mar-12	Cheltenham	1.87	2.1	Yes	12.30
28-Jan-12	Cheltenham	1.3	1.66	Yes	27.69
17-Dec-11	Ascot	1.33	1.67	Yes	25.56
26-Nov-11	Newbury	1.16	1.35	Yes	16.38
07-Apr-11	Aintree	1.73	1.76	Yes	1.73
17-Mar-11	Cheltenham	2.04	2.84	Yes	39.22
29-Dec-10	Newbury	1.18	1.19	Yes	0.85
27-Nov-10	Newbury	1.3	1.33	Yes	2.31
08-Apr-10	Aintree	1.34	1.56	Yes	16.42
18-Mar-10	Cheltenham	1.96	2.02	Yes	3.06
29-Dec-09	Newbury	1.52	5	Yes	228.95
28-Nov-09	Newbury	1.41	1.41	No	0.00
02-Apr-09	Aintree	1.86	2.8	Yes	50.54
12-Mar-09	Cheltenham	7.4	9.8	Yes	32.43
24-Jan-09	Cheltenham	4.74	40	Yes	743.88
01-Jan-09	Cheltenham	6.4	7	Yes	9.37

Figure 15.0

As you can see, he traded at a higher price in fifteen of the eighteen races so it really was a case of simply laying him pre-race and backing him in-running (although you will notice that in his latest two races his price never went above SP so perhaps this strategy had run its course on *Big Buck's*). I'm not going to claim any great credit for coming up with this strategy, it's pretty simple stuff. But just because it's simple doesn't mean it's easy — and coming up with the selections to trade is definitely the hard part as it proves quite time-consuming. Perhaps *Big Buck's* is a poor example as he's an absolute freak of a horse and actually won each of the races listed above, but he's a horse that will be known to many readers so he illustrates my point perfectly. *Big Buck's* has now retired but will be remembered fondly by many.

Initially, I decided to focus on horses like *Big Buck's* that often got bored mid-race but always had plenty in the tank when push came to shove. I'd lay first and back later but I then ran into the problem of large liabilities on horses with bigger prices, thus over-exposing my account. It was OK with short-priced selections like *Big Buck's* but when it came to bigger-priced horses, I was leaving myself open. If my stake was £10 for example, and my selection was priced 20.0, this meant that I'd have a liability of £190 on that horse alone. A few such selections on a busy Saturday would leave me exposed to some serious losses if something went wrong but it also tied up a lot of capital which I needed for other bets and trades. With this type of inplay trading, stop-losses don't always work too well. Of course, I could have adjusted the stakes to match the price of the horses but as it happened, I wasn't always around to place the bets when testing out this strategy (due to other work commitments). Instead, I had a spreadsheet linked to Gruss Software automatically laying the bets for me at Betfair SP and then trading out for a pre-defined percentage rise in the price inplay. For example, I'd lay at Betfair SP and back in-running if the price rose 50% higher than the Betfair SP. This strategy had a high strike rate of course (in a ten runner race, nine of the horses are going to lose and therefore rise in price) but it was the occasional trades which went badly that really hurt the bank. On one occasion, I lost a monkey (£500) in the space of twenty minutes on two horses that never rose in price and I knew then it was time to change tack. I'd also lost a big sum two days earlier and it was all becoming far too stressful and costly.

As I say, when I began this strategy, I couldn't be at the computer all day to monitor my liabilities as I was working on some non-betting related projects. I needed to find a way where I could risk a certain amount per trade so instead of laying first, I decided to back first. But because I was backing first, this meant that I would no longer be looking for horses that hit a flat spot or ran poorly mid race; I was now looking for horses that tend to *run well* mid-race (thus shortening in price) but not actually win. I'll explain later with examples.

Ideally, the horse would run well enough to see its price drop by 50% at which point I would lay, using **double the back stake**. Then hopefully, the horse would run out of steam and lose the race so I could keep the lay stake. This became the new strategy. So to simplify, I now:

• Back the selection at Betfair SP
• Hope that the selection runs well mid-race

- Lay the selection if it hits half its Betfair SP inplay (using double the back stake)
- Hope the horse runs out of gas in the final stages of the race and loses

One simple thing to remember: Betfair use decimal odds. People often forget this and a certain mistake is very common. Say a horse goes off at 11.0 for example, and you want to lay it inplay for half its price: some people would try to lay it at 5.5 which would be the wrong thing to do. A price drop of 50% on an 11.0 horse is actually 6.0. It becomes clearer when you convert to fractional odds. As you know, 11.0 is 10/1 in fractional odds and half of 10/1 is 5/1. Converted back to decimal, the 5/1 becomes 6.0. Perhaps this is obvious to you but I thought it worth mentioning as I've actually seen a few people make this mistake. Anyway, back to the strategy...

EXAMPLE ONE

On 12th April 2012, the Donald McCain-trained *Tara Royal* was entered for a handicap chase at Aintree.

I'd checked his formbook comments for clues to his running style and found various pointers to suggest that he might run well, but not actually win. There are numerous places where you can check a horse's running style. Personally, I like to use Timeform but I know people who use other sources such as the *Racing Post*, *Sporting Life* or Raceform Interactive to get the information they need. Comments such as *had every chance, in touch, making headway, tracked the leaders* etc. are the type of thing I'm looking for as they indicate that the horse looked like he was doing well before losing. Horses that appear to be doing well usually see their prices drop. And certain horses have a running style which they tend to repeat time and time again.

Next, I went to the Timeform/Betfair website where you can check back on a horse's Betfair SP and how high or low it traded at inplay in its past races. It's a great resource and doesn't cost a penny. From this page, I could tell that *Tara Royal* went off at 44.86 in its previous race at the Cheltenham Festival and traded as low as 6.40 inplay which is a drop of 84%. A month earlier, he went off at 6.61 at Musselburgh in a race he actually won. Before that, he went off at 13.5 in a race at Doncaster in January and hit a low of 6.0 which is a drop of 60%. And two weeks previous, he went off at 20.0 at Warwick and traded at 2.6 inplay, a drop of 92%. There were further examples of price drops as I went through his record which I won't list here but I hope you get the picture by now. Generally, I'll take the horse's latest six races into consideration although it's no harm to go back further if you have time.

Finally, I watched a few videos of his previous races just to confirm what I'd noted down. This type of race-watching can be time-consuming and I'm often tempted to skip it. However, sometimes a horse's price can drop inplay for reasons other than its running style (the favourite might fall for example). I prefer to be sure that it's the horses running style that saw it trade lower, rather than a random event — so the race-watching is necessary.

Having decided that *Tara Royal*'s running style suggested that he was likely to trade at a lower price inplay, I backed him with £100. His Betfair SP was 17.87 and once the race went inplay, I put in my order to lay the horse at half of that price. The lay stake was £200. I sit it out and hope my judgement was correct. At this point, there are three possible outcomes:

- If *Tara Royal*'s price doesn't drop to 50% of its Betfair SP, I lose my £100 back stake.

- If *Tara Royal* wins the race, I will win £1687 for my £100 back bet at Betfair SP but lose as much for my £200 lay bet at half the Betfair SP. In other words, I don't win or lose any money. I like to call these 'level' trades.

- If *Tara Royal*'s price drops below 50% of its Betfair SP but the horse goes on to lose the race, I will lose £100 on the back bet, but gain £200 on the lay bet. This is the desired outcome as it leaves me £100 in profit.

If we exclude the level trades (which don't win or lose any money), we are left with a situation where I'll either win £100 or lose £100. I like the simplicity in this and it brings me back to the earlier point about trading being a zero-sum game — someone wins and someone loses, just like the old days in the bookies. Again, if we exclude the level bets, it's really a case of getting my strike rate above 50% over time in which case I'll show a profit because I'm effectively betting at even money (excluding commission).

Anyway, getting back to the *Tara Royal* example: as mentioned, he went off at 17.87 and I put in an order to lay him at half that price, using double my back stake. He hit a low of 5.0 during that race so my order was matched — but he finished up in ninth place which netted me £100 before commission.

EXAMPLE TWO
On 20th February 2012, I spotted the Paul Nicholls trained *Do It For Dalkey* entered in a handicap race at Carlisle. I checked his formbook comments, his previous inplay prices and I also watched a number of his past races. I was satisfied that he was likely to trade at a low price in running so I put in an order to back him at his Betfair SP with £100. He went off at 5.10 and I put in my £200 lay order at 3.05 but unfortunately, he only traded at a low of 4.40 (a drop of 17%) meaning my lay bet was left unmatched. The net result was that I lost the back stake of £100.

EXAMPLE THREE
On 12th April 2010, *Naked Cowboy* was running in an Irish flat race at Gowran Park. Using the methods listed earlier, I'd identified him as one that was likely to trade at a low price inplay so I backed him with £100 at a Betfair SP of 6.32. I then put in my counter lay for £200 at half that price. *Naked Cowboy* actually went on to win that race so I won £532 for my back bet, but lost as much on the lay. So this was a 'level trade' where I didn't win or lose any money.

IS THIS TEACHABLE?
As mentioned, I wasn't going to include this chapter as it's not exactly a strategy that can be taught easily as there is no systematic way to come up with the selections. Readers will have to forgive me if some parts are a bit vague but race-reading is not really something one can teach in a book and it's best to try it for yourself to see if you have a knack for it. I often wonder if

having a knowledge of horseracing is a help or a hindrance when it comes to trading. When you are familiar with the horses, it can cloud your judgement when trading as you can make certain assumptions about how its price will go but in this strategy, some knowledge of the formbook is essential. Everyone who watches a horse's past race will interpret it differently and if two people were to sit down and look at the daily runners, it is unlikely that they will come up with the same list of horses to trade. It's also something I've only been working on for a relatively short time and while it's been successful thus far, I've only got a few hundred trades under the belt so I can't be certain that it will remain successful. Nonetheless, this book is all about ideas and perhaps some readers may find it useful, so I guess there's no harm in including it. It can be tricky at first but with a bit of practice, I don't see why anyone can't figure out a horse's running style. It does take time, but I feel I'm getting better at it as I gain more experience. Personally, I like to lay at 50% of the in-running price as it keeps things simple but more importantly, it has proven the most profitable level to trade at so far. That's the thing about keeping good records; I can back-test various scenarios using different stakes or different prices to see what works best.

While this strategy is time-consuming, so far it has paid off. I'm making no bold claims about it yet though, and it comes with all the usual health warnings. One thing that traders may find a little awkward (especially if they have a full-time job) is the fact that they have to be sitting at a computer at certain times to place the trades. People who have to be out and about each day usually only have set times in which they can trade — and this strategy doesn't allow for that flexibility as the selections may be running at any time during the week. However as mentioned earlier, with the help of Gruss Betting Assistant I've been able to get an Excel spreadsheet set up which has automated the process. If I'm not going to be at the computer all day, I can now set up the spreadsheet in the morning, type in my selections and stakes, and leave it running while I'm out. On one occasion, this had disastrous consequences when the missus unwittingly shut down the computer mid-race. That episode cost me a couple of ton and but for the fact that I'm Catholic, I think divorce papers would have been served! Now, I stick a rather large 'do not turn off' sign on the computer if I'm out and about for the day. If you are doing this manually, you have to be quick off the mark getting your counter-lay in, especially in the flat sprint races which are over in a flash. Whether or not the time and effort I put into this strategy continues to pay off remains to be seen but if you have some knowledge of the sport, it could be something worth trying for yourself. I'd also be interested to hear from any readers who have managed to adapt this strategy for other sports.

MOMENTUM SWING TRADING

Men, it has been well said, think in herds; it will be seen that they go mad in herds, while they only recover their senses slowly, and one by one — Charles Mackay, author of *'Extraordinary Popular Delusions and the Madness of Crowds'*, first published in 1841

FROM the late 1990s right through to the financial crash of 2007, you couldn't go to a pub, a party or indeed any sort of social gathering in Ireland without hearing someone talk about property prices. The price of houses became a national obsession and everyone became desperate to get on the property ladder. The banks were only too happy to accommodate and relaxed their lending rules to allow for 100% mortgages with scant regard for the future and whether or not the applicants would be able to keep up the repayments. It was all a massive bubble and it popped with devastating consequences. As a nation, we are now living with the fallout. Pay cuts, redundancies, repossessions and emigration are now the topics of the day in Ireland and it will take a generation before the mess is finally cleaned up.

I won't pretend to be one of those that predicted the crash before it happened but I did watch in disbelief as the prices of houses in Ballybrack, the small working-class suburb of Dublin in which I grew up, went through the roof. In 2004, my daughter was born and then aged 24, I was feeling the social pressure to get my act together and buy a home for my new little family. But I just couldn't bring myself to fork out half a million quid for a three bedroom semi-d in Ballybrack, when I had seen those same houses for sale for sixty or seventy grand as a teenager just a decade earlier. For years, my wife and I waited for house prices to level out but they just went up and up for a considerable length of time.

Yes, the bubble did burst; they all do eventually — but the point I'm making here is that trends often last far longer than we anticipate. I never would have thought that prices would keep rising year-on-year for a decade but due to the herd mentality, they did just that. The funny thing is, the opposite has occurred since 2007 as prices now plummet. For the past six years, we have had economists on TV telling us that prices are about to bottom out but at the time of writing, prices are down over 50% on their peak in places, and outside of the capital city Dublin, they are still falling. When prices were rising, everyone kept expecting them to level out but it took more than a decade to do so. Similarly, when prices started to slide, everyone seemed to think they would bottom out quickly but once again, it seems that people are underestimating the strength of the trend. In summary, prices rose for a much longer period than people predicted — and prices are now falling for a much longer period than people predicted.

How does this relate to trading? Well, let me come back to the old clichéd phrase 'the trend is your friend'. It may be old advice but generally speaking, it is better to swim with the tide than against it. If the price of something is rising and a trend is established, it's more likely to continue in that direction than reverse. It's our job to hop on for just part of the journey and make some money along the way. The beauty of trend following is that you don't have to know or worry too much about the fundamentals of whatever it is you are trading. If it's a stock price, you don't have to know too much about the company. If it's a horse, you don't have to concern yourself with why the price is drifting or steaming. Just recognise the fact, and jump on for some of the ride.

When trend following, some people become obsessed with buying and selling right at the top and bottom of the market but it's almost impossible to get it right and I've found that it's best not to stress about that too much. Rather, jump on the trend as it is in motion, collect some money along the way and then jump off. **Making money is our goal, not perfection**. Think of it like a train journey to work. Very few people get on at the very first stop on the line and then get off at the last. Most people get on for a few stops along the way and then get off again. Just like trading, they hop on for part of the journey, get some benefit from doing so, and then hop off again.

MARKET MOVERS

If a price is rising or dropping sharply, is it more likely to continue in that direction?

If we look at the price of anything (horses, football teams, stocks, houses) at a given moment in time, we are given a summary of how the market feels about the product in question. In theory at least, the price has a fifty percent chance of going up and a fifty percent chance of going down. Efficient market theory tells us that all known information is built into the price at that given time. But theory and practice are often two different things and there are times when the likelihood of the price rising or falling is not exactly 50:50. In my many years as a horseracing punter, I noticed that a drifter or a steamer in the market is more likely to continue in the direction it is going rather than reversing. This information will not be new to anyone who has tried to back a horse on-course or online in a fast-moving market while the price is getting smashed in quickly. By the time you get your money out of your wallet to hand to the bookie, the price may have shortened up even further. **Markets that are trending (moving strongly in a certain direction) are more likely to continue to move in that direction.**

While it may not be big news to punters, this information is highly useful to traders. Take a few moments to digest the following statement:

In a proper trending market, it is more likely than not that the price will continue in the direction it has been trading in hitherto. These markets can be identified and traded.

In other words, certain markets are somewhat predictable. That simple statement, if true, is tremendous news for traders. Now throughout this book, you will notice that I have said that most markets are unpredictable and that you don't need to know which way the market is going to move in order to make money — so I can see why including a trend-following strategy in this book may seem contradictory. But while I do stand by my original assessment that most markets are random, an exception is made for trending markets.

MOMENTUM

In his highly informative book *Taming the Lion: 100 Secret Strategies for Investing*, the well-known private investor and Dragon's Den star Richard Farleigh discusses a trends-based investing strategy which works across commodities, currencies, interest rates, stocks and property. I've adapted

Farleigh's strategy for the sports trading markets and to my delight, have found that it works there too. Some years back, Farleigh and his team ran computer tests using historical data on a broad range of markets:

'We compared how often markets continued in an existing direction to how often they went into reverse. In theory, the results should be around 50:50 for continuations versus reversals. However, the exciting news was that the results showed an average of around 55% continuations to 45% reversals, which is a very strong bias. The difference is a percentage of net winners: 10%.

...when a market is trending up, it is more likely to rise further than it is to fall. Equally, when it is trending down, it is more likely to fall further than it is to rise...

Now what do I mean by trending up and trending down? I mean that a market has had a fairly smooth rise or fall by a meaningful amount. A small move of one or two per cent does not define a trend. These moves may be just 'noise' in the market, caused by the random actions of a few buyers or sellers. A trend requires a more meaningful move, such as five or ten per cent....

Trends remain the easiest trading advantage that I have ever come across...

As I have mentioned, the average bias towards the trend direction is about 10%. This may seem like a small number, but it is extremely important — remember that even a small advantage like this is enough to help us tremendously.'

So as Farleigh points out, trends are a huge advantage to traders.

Forgive me for straying away from sports trading for the moment but the aforementioned house price bubble in Ireland illustrates my point perfectly about the power of trend following. Now I must point out that I'm taking plenty of liberties with Farleigh's strategy here and adapting it broadly to suit my own purposes — but take a look at the below chart (figure 16.0) which shows the average price of a house in Dublin from 2004 to 2012:

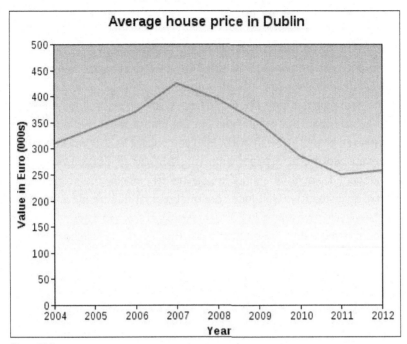

Figure 16.0

Let's take 2004, the year I started looking at buying a house as a starting point for this graph. It was also a time when prices really started to take off. Back then, the price of a house in Dublin was €310,000. Keep in mind that this house-price graph is essentially no different from any other type of product or price that you can buy and sell, including the price of a horse or football team etc. on the betting exchanges. By 2005, house prices had risen to €340,000. Would they continue to rise? It's easy to look back on a graph now and say 'yes' but back then we couldn't be certain. As my father used to say, "If hindsight were foresight, we'd all be millionaires".

One think we could tell in 2005 though, was that the market was trending (it had moved by a meaningful amount) so there was a slightly greater chance that the prices would continue to rise rather than decline. Now you could, of course, come back to me with plenty of examples where the prices do not continue in the direction and your examples may be correct. But I'm not saying that it works all of the time — as outlined by Farleigh, trending markets average around 55% continuations to 45% reversals. You will have plenty of losing trades too, but over time you should have an edge.

The price rise from €310,000 to €340,000 is a change of about 9.7%. Farleigh defines a trending market as one that has moved by around five or ten percent so in this case, I would say that house prices are a 'buy' in 2005 as they had moved by a meaningful amount. House prices continued to rise and peaked at €425,000 in 2007. Had you bought in 2005 at €340,000, you were looking at a paper profit of €85,000 in 2007. However as mentioned, it would be almost impossible to pinpoint the height of the market so instead, we wait for a confirmation that that trend has reversed before we sell. A year later in 2008, prices were down to €395,000 which is a drop of more than 7% on their peak. That 7% drop could be described as a meaningful amount so at this stage, we recognise that we may be in a downtrend and sell. The end result of all of this is that we buy at €340,000 and sell at €395,000. It's true to say that we would have missed out on a better opportunity to sell in 2007 but trying to predict when prices are at their peak is, in my opinion, a pointless exercise and relies on pure luck. By following trends, you do miss the tops and bottoms but you can still make some money by hitching a ride along the way. As you can see from the graph, the trend continued and prices were down at €250,000 in 2011. By 2012, they had recovered by a modest 3.2% but as yet, this is not enough to convince me that the tide has turned back upwards although it's one I watch with interest. Buying and selling houses is, of course, a bit more complicated than the above but now that you understand the concept, let's get back to business and look at an example from the betting exchanges.

SPOTTING THE TREND

Firstly, the thing to remember with the betting exchanges is that prices are in decimal so remember to take away one. Figure 16.1, shows the betting on *Gabrials Hope* from a race at Wolverhampton (15th February 2013):

If we ignore the initial squiggles on the chart which are the early low-volume fluctuations, we can see that the price for *Gabrials Hope* stalls briefly around 8.0 (which was around 15 minutes before the off). This price of

Wolv 15th Feb - 1m6f Hcap

Betting on: Gabrials Hope ▾
Total matched on this event: €44,556
Reduction Factor 16.7%
Betting summary - Volume: €10,371
Last price matched: 6.20
Projected Betfair Starting Price: 5.38907

Price/Volume over time

Inverse Axis

Figure 16.1

8.0 is what I call the 'starting point' and it's the first thing we need to find. The starting point is simply the point from which we are going to monitor the price and wait for a trend. Generally speaking, your starting point is when the market begins to get busy. In this case, the previous race had just finished so lots of traders and punters were opening up this market. In the big racing festivals such as the Derby meeting, Cheltenham Festival or Aintree Grand National meeting, the starting point begins earlier and the markets may already be trading serious volumes before 10 a.m. on the morning of the race. But for the day-to-day meetings involving low-grade racing, there's rarely any serious money around until 10-15 minutes before the off. It takes a bit of practice to identify a starting point for a price and it's certainly not an exact science — but after a while, you should get a feel for when other participants are entering a market. As I say, on the low-grade meetings, the starting point for monitoring a price is usually 10-15 minutes before the off or else when the previous race has ended.

Having decided to start monitoring the price at 8.0 (7/1), we then simply wait on the market to take its direction. Like most strategies in this book, the beauty here is that you don't have to predict which way the price is going to go. You simply wait on your signal to enter. In this case, our signal to enter is when the price has risen or fallen from the 8.0 staring point by a significant amount (5-10%).

As you can see from the chart, the price quickly drops down from 8.0, so I get in with a back bet which is matched at 7.6, a move of nearly 6%. I'm now hoping the trend continues downwards. At this point, I should mention stop-losses. In this strategy, my initial stop-loss is the original price I got involved with (in this case 8.0) and I will manually adjust that stop-loss if the trade progresses in my favour. My stops in this particular strategy are never set in stone. I manually move them in the direction of the trade if the trade is going my way. I suppose you could loosely describe it as a *manual trailing stop*.

The price continues to go with the flow and falls down to 6.0. As expected, it meets some resistance at 6.0 as this is a major crossover point (see chapter four) and stalls for a moment. I am given some breathing space (for a few seconds) so now is a good time to re-evaluate my position. I decide that I don't want to lose any money on this trade so I move my stop-loss down to my entry point of 7.6. This is a nice position to be in as I can simply reap any rewards that now come my way without any pressure.

Next, the price bounces off 6.0 and moves up to 6.8. This all happens quite quickly so I now must decide what to do. The move from 6.0 to 6.8 is nearly 15%. A move of 15% is significant and could mean that the trend is now on an upswing so it may be time to get out. However, also playing on my mind at this point is the fact that we often get a bounce at the key prices such as 6.0. Is it a bounce? Is it an uptrend? These are the split second decisions that must be made. I move my stop-loss to 7.2 just in case we have entered an uptrend. If so, I will get stopped out at 7.2 but still retain some profit. As it happens, the price briefly touches 7.0 before dropping back down to 6.2. It was just a bounce. At this stage, you can see (around the middle of the chart) that the price is 'in a range' and seems to be stuck around 6.2 and 6.4. Trading in a range (sideways) is a signal that the main price move is over so I exit my trade at 6.2. As it happens, I probably got out too early as the market breaks down past 6.0 to 5.8 for a time. It eventually settles around 6.0 at the off. However, I've made my profit and I can move on to the next race.

THE PROFITABLE, NON-PERFECT TRADE

I backed at 7.6 and layed at 6.2 which earned me a profit of around seven pips. Did I back at the top of the market and lay at the bottom? No, I didn't — so you could say that I missed out on some profit. But I don't care as I made my money along the way and it was quite stress-free as I had sensible stop-losses in place. We are not striving for the perfect trade, we are just looking to make some money. I used to drive myself mad with trades like the above considering all the 'what ifs' and bemoaning the fact that I didn't get the maximum value out of the swing. But I now realise that it's not all about pinpointing the exact turning point and I'm happy to hop on for just part of the journey.

Discipline is required in all types of trading but particularly for momentum swing trading where the temptation is there to hang around for too long. While he may have been discussing financial trading rather than sports trading, Alexander Elder sums up the mindset required for momentum trading very well in his book Come Into My Trading Room:

'Successful momentum trading requires great discipline. You must identify a price move, hop aboard without waiting for a better confirmation, and jump off as soon as that move slows down. The longer you wait to identify *the momentum, the less money is left for you. Taking profits is stressful because of a normal human tendency to hold out for a little more and then beat yourself up for having left too early. A momentum trader needs a set of technical rules, a money management system, and iron discipline to enter when the time is right and exit without regrets after hitting his profit target or a loss limit.'*

Elder later goes on to say that momentum trading appears deceptively easy but is harder than it looks. Note his important comments about momentum trading being a boring business:

'Momentum trading has a built-in psychological contradiction that's deadly to most people. On the one hand, this fast game, like infantry fighting or video game playing, is best suited to young people with strong hunting instincts, capable of abandoning themselves to the game. On the other hand, momentum trading requires the cold detached discipline of a professional card counter at a casino. Successful momentum trading, like professional gambling, is a boring business. The ability to accept small steady gains — essential for momentum trading — is very rare. Few people can walk away from the table just as the party gets going.'

Forget about making every trade textbook perfect, being a good trader is not about getting everything faultless. I'm not saying that you shouldn't strive to be the best trader you can possibly be — all I'm saying is that if you focus on getting it perfect every time, you will miss out on good opportunities to make money such as in the above scenario. Accept the fact that you will leave money on the table, accept the fact that you will rarely hit the top or bottom of the market and accept that fact that you will get stopped out sometimes. There's no such thing as a perfect trader — but great traders are the ones who know they can still make money without having to buy at the top and sell at the bottom every time.

PUTTING IT ALL TOGETHER

Luck is what happens when preparation meets opportunity — Seneca
(c. 4 BC — 65 AD), Roman philosopher and playwright

THIS chapter is not so much about any particular strategy — it's more general hints, tips and thoughts about trading for those that have a bank ready and want to give it a go. I think it's one of the most important chapters of the book nonetheless, and I hope it helps readers avoid some of the silly costly mistakes I made in the past. It also includes some general thoughts and tips that didn't fit in elsewhere. The last chapter in the book discusses setting up a trading plan which, I believe, is a central step in becoming a successful trader.

YOU WILL LOSE, AND LOSE, AND LOSE
Losing many times over is part and parcel of trading and it can't be avoided. That's a simple statement of fact but getting used to that idea is a lot easier said than done. Losing is painful and psychological research using functional magnetic resonance imaging (fMRI) on the brain shows that the intensity of emotion is far greater when we lose money than it is when we gain it. If we could measure happiness on a plus and minus scale, the amount of 'happiness points' your mood goes up when you win £100 is around half as many as the amount of points your mood goes down when you lose £100. In other words, losses stir stronger emotions than gains. This is an important fact that you need to be aware of because when we are extremely emotional, we are more likely to stray from our trading plan (discussed in chapter nineteen). If you are trying out a certain strategy, you need to have a rough idea of what your likely losing run might be. If you are doing one tick scalping for example, it would be upsetting (although certainly not impossible) to get ten trades wrong. But if you were looking for a large move which earns you twenty pips or more for example, it would be perfectly acceptable to have, say, eight losers in a row before hitting your trade. Ask yourself what the strike rate of your strategy is. If you don't know the answer, you haven't done enough research and testing. Research

should be done with small stakes on every strategy you try until you have a meaningful amount of data built up. This is why it's extremely important to record everything you are doing in a spreadsheet. Get to grips with Excel and keep on building your data. So many people make the mistake of jumping from market to market and trying different strategies on each but, as boring as it is, the only real way to become an expert in any given strategy is to do it over and over and over and over, all the time recording information in Excel about each trade. It can be as tedious as hell, especially if you are only using small stakes but going at the market with a load of dosh and a few half-learned strategies is not going to work. Some people seem to think that using a bigger bank will help them become successful but if you can't profit consistently with a small bank, you won't do it with a big one. So many people fail to realise this. You need to become an expert in one or two strategies before moving on to another. Remember too that not all strategies will work for you and some won't suit your personality. I'm getting better as the years go by but I still find swing trading strategies which involve lots of small losses and then one big win difficult, and prefer the good feeling that comes from lots of little wins (with the odd big loss). Everyone is different and you need to find your style. If you are following the strategies in this book, make sure you have adapted them to suit your needs and mastered them with small stakes before going at the markets with big money. I don't want any nasty emails telling me how you lost money following the advice contained in this book — if it's not working for you with small change, don't try it with big money. Remember, these are just pointers to help you out — you still need to learn to get a feel for the markets so it would be very foolish to start off with a substantial amount of money as not all strategies will suit your personality. I've taught a number of people these strategies and even though they've all received the same training, their trading results are wildly different. In fact, you can give a group of people the exact same set of rules to follow on a single strategy and they will still come back with different results. Why is this so? Well, it's like being in school — we were all taught the same curriculum but some people in the class were better at grasping the concepts than others. Most of us were good at some subjects but poorer at others. In trading, you not only have to grasp the concepts but you have to spot them and then apply them in a fast-moving, highly charged and often emotional environment. With so many personality types out there, it's inevitable that some people will find certain strategies in this book a great help while some will still be left staring at the screen wondering why they are losing. As I say, the message here is to master one or two strategies with small stakes before moving on to another or increasing your stake size. You will lose plenty of times along the way but if you have proper data gathered, you have a good idea if a particular losing streak is perfectly normal or whether it is something out of the ordinary.

REACTING TO NEGATIVE EVENTS

I wish I had thought more about this long ago; it would have saved me thousands of Euros. Most of us know one or two people who always seem to have bad luck follow them around. They never win the prize, they never get the promotion, they never get ahead — and life seems to deal them one bad hand after another. It could be a colleague, it could be a family member, it could be your spouse — indeed, maybe even you are one of those seemingly hapless individuals. Always the victim of circumstance. But very often, a good chunk of that 'bad luck' is brought on by the person themselves. You might be wondering what the hell does this have to do with trading but the answer is 'a lot'. Everyone will have random negative events in their life including traders; it's just part and parcel of being a human being. Sometimes those events will be devastating and there will be little you can do about it (getting into a debilitating accident for example), but on the whole, we normally have choices on how we react to an event, including negative events. And I believe it's how we react to negative events in our life (and trading) which will determine our general level of success. Don't get me wrong here, I'm not one for all that 'law of attraction' nonsense but it is true to say that those people who view the world in a positive way and learn from mistakes do that bit better for themselves in life.

I once had a friend who could never seem to land a decent job, even when the economy was on fire and jobs were aplenty. He often felt like a victim of life and would blame everyone else when the interview wouldn't go his way. On the face of it, he had a good case; he was highly qualified and was prepared to work but he just never got a call back after the interview. I used to pity him but then one day I met him on the morning of an interview and his demeanour explained it all. He was tired, he hadn't shaved and was generally downbeat. He felt he wasn't going to get the job anyway as he was an 'unlucky person' so hadn't made much effort. I certainly wouldn't have given him a job. This same clown was in the pub later feeling sorry for himself and telling anyone who would listen how he had, yet again, been the victim and couldn't find a job. Had he scrubbed up well and gone in with a beaming smile, he probably would have nailed it. Again, I don't mean to sound patronising or like one of those American self-help gurus, but a little effort goes a long way.

Conversely, there are people in this world that appear to be 'lucky' and everything goes their way. While it's true that all successful people owe part of their success to luck and being in the right place at the right time, I believe that most successful people were simply prepared when an opportunity arose and they took it. Yes, some people get rich by pure blind luck and no talent — just look at any reality TV show at the moment. But for the rest of us, the old adage 'the harder I work, the luckier I get' sums it up perfectly. People sometimes appear 'lucky' to the outside world but you'll find in many cases that they had put in the work in their chosen field, remained positive when things went wrong, and were therefore able to spot the opportunities that 'unlucky' people would let pass them by. Not every opportunity will work out but people that have put in the work and are willing to try things out will find other opportunities, some of which may work well. By not acting the victim and accepting that your success in life (or lack of) right now is more or less down to your attitude and decisions hitherto is the only way to go. Taking responsibility for yourself, accepting that both good and bad things happen at random, and not blaming the outside world for a lack of success can actually be quite refreshing.

As I say, this all applies to trading too. Playing the victim cost me thousands of Euros early in my trading career. Playing the victim allowed me to have a reason to chase my losses. An example might be when I would back a horse hoping to lay it at a shorter price — but then something unusual happened which caused the price to drift (such as the horse getting distressed approaching the starting stalls). The proper way to react to this situation would have been to take my loss and move on. However, I would feel like events had transpired against me and that I was entitled to 'get my money back' and get back on an even keel. So I might let the trade go inplay (which is pure gambling) or chase it on the next trade. But chasing the loss often saw me dig a deeper hole for myself and all of a sudden I'd be facing a very big loss, often in the hundreds. Again, instead of just accepting what had happened and learning from it, the victim voice in my head would say "You've been hit with double bad luck, not only did a random event scupper your trade, the loss chasing didn't work out. You are now down €500 and it's barely your fault". Instead of accepting my fate, I'd then go and have a €500 bet on something at even money just to get the money back and make everything seem right in the world. When I'd place the bet, I'd promise myself each time that I would never chase losses again; I only needed to do it this once because of the 'unlucky' string of events. 'This time it is different', I would convince myself. However, those are possibly the most dangerous five words of all when it comes to trading. Sometimes the loss chasing would work, but other times it wouldn't and all of a sudden, I'd be down a grand. I'm ashamed to admit, I've chased losses even bigger than that on more than one occasion often with disastrous consequences. Within minutes, you can find yourself down a couple of grand all because you wouldn't accept a relatively small loss at the start. Once you are in this situation, it's extremely hard, almost impossible in fact, to stop chasing it. You may chase it and get it back the odd time but inevitably, you will wipe out your account. And I've done that more than once.

Here's what you have to get your head around: unusual things happen in trading and sometimes they cause a trade to go good or bad. It's as simple as that. But simple as that statement might be, it's not so easy to accept when it happens.

Be wary too when people say that 'everything happens for a reason'. Have you ever noticed that people mostly say this when bad things happen? If you find yourself saying this about trading, it means you are making excuses for yourself and trying to find comfort. People often say things like:

'It'll work out best in the end', but again, they are simply looking to comfort themselves from a difficult situation. These sayings are fine and can offer compassion in the right circumstances but this type of thinking has no place in trading. We do it in our own heads too and comfort ourselves when we make a mistake. But this just shelters us from reality. Today, instead of saying 'things happen for a reason', I'd rather simply say 'things happen'. And when things happen, both good and bad, I deal with it as best I can. This applies to life as well as trading. My mantra now is 'things happen, and I will deal with it'.

In trading, you need this mindset; you need to be able to step away when something goes wrong, observe what happened, and say to yourself objectively. "Oh, that's interesting. One of those random things have happened. I'd better close out my trade". When a random event causes you to make money, don't get excited and play with that money. You need that same cold attitude. Close out your trade, bank the money and get back to what you were doing. Some people feel an urge to gamble or play up this money as they 'wouldn't have had it anyway' but if you do that, you don't respect your money. Remember, this 'lucky' money may be needed to compensate for an 'unlucky' loss later on. Money earned, even if it is through an accident, is your money and **every penny is a prisoner** in this game. Money can be given and taken away unexpectedly in trading and it's something you have to get used to. Bank it and move on when you happen to be on the good side of it. Cut your losses and move on when you are on the bad side of it. It sounds simple but the human brain can work in weird ways. Don't play the victim — if you are allowing yourself to chase a loss FOR ANY REASON, you've lost the plot.

Here's the thing about trading: It exposes you to your deep-down self. And to be honest, sometimes it's not nice to meet our deep-down self. We spend most of our daily lives projecting an image of how we wish others to perceive us. After a while, you may even begin to believe that this is the 'real' you. But the market strips away all that bullshit. When you trade, any flaws you have, any impulses, greediness, fears, weaknesses, will be brought to the surface, no matter how hard you try to hide them. Remember the Seven Deadly Sins? Certainly in my trading career, I have in some way or other succumbed to lust, gluttony, greed, sloth, wrath, envy and pride. It sounds like a tired old cliché but to be a good trader, you have to know yourself. And that includes the bad sides which we normally hide from the world and ourselves. Above all, you have to know your weaknesses and don't let the markets exploit them. Because the markets will try to do so at every available opportunity.

GIVING BACK TO THE MARKET

As mentioned, you will have plenty of losers along the way and this is difficult to take, but if you never gave any money back to the market, why would the other participants return? For you to win, someone else has to lose but losers won't return if they get beaten up by the market every single time. If you have your strategy right, you should make money over time and the money you make from winning trades should cover your losses overall. Think of it like you are a casino owner. It's almost impossible to beat the house in the longer term yet people go back and back for more. The roulette wheel, for example, allows for lots of small wins and offers hope to the gambler sitting there betting on black or red. Some days, the customer will win and if the customer keeps his gambling under control it can make for a great evening out with friends. On logic, no-one should play a game like roulette where the odds are automatically stacked against you before you begin but the possibility of making some easy money is very attractive and people keep coming back for more. Do you think the casino owner gets upset when a customer wins money on a particular spin? Of course not, he knows he will make money over time. A customer may even be on a so-called 'winning streak' but the casino owner will not be worried at all. He knows that he needs to let his customers have winning days from time to time in order to see them return. Can you imagine a casino which never lost a bet? It would be a pretty empty place. It's like that with trading. The people you are taking money from are other exchange users. If those other exchange users didn't win money from time to time, they wouldn't stay around. As mentioned before, this is (more or less) a zero-sum game where someone wins and someone loses and the betting exchanges would become a very lonely place if only one side won the money. If there are no other customers, there's no way to make money. Those customers who lose overall must be thrown a bone now and then and given a bit of hope or else they won't return. Try to remember the casino owner analogy the next time you find yourself getting upset about a string of losing trades. Successful gamblers can see the long-term picture while unsuccessful punters get far too emotional over every individual win and loss. As I said before, the most important thing is to **stay in the game**. Don't stake too big. Keep some money so you can live to fight another day.

BAD OLD BANKS — A WORD OF CAUTION

A good number of years ago, I went to my bank for a loan of about €500 to help pay for a holiday. I assumed I would get it no problem as I had been a customer there ever since my business studies teacher sent me down as a teenager to open a bank account for my homework in the early 90s. I had a small but regular wage coming in from a part-time job, I hadn't got much debt and I had never been overdrawn on my account. I also had €200 in savings with the bank so I reckoned getting a loan for such a small amount would be a mere formality. About two days after I sent in the forms, the postman arrived with a letter and I assumed it contained a cheque. But there was no cheque inside — it was a loan refusal letter. I got on the blower to the bank (this was back in the days when you could still pick up the phone and speak to a human in your local branch) and they told me the reason my loan was refused was because there were some gambling transactions in the past few months on my statement. I was shocked. Over the previous year, I had deposited about €200 with a bookmaker. I lost about €100 at first but then through some blind dumb luck on Saturday afternoon, I had a football bet come up and earned about €300 — so I decided to withdraw the lot from the account which was roughly €400. Despite the fact that I had deposited €200 and withdrawn €400 (a total profit of €200), the bank saw this as a bad thing and put a notice on my account that I could be a 'risky' person when it came to loans. I later heard about someone who was refused a mortgage because of some gambling transactions on his otherwise impeccable account. This was a very serious situation for the guy as he had to go home and explain to his wife that they couldn't buy a home because he decided to have a pony on the favourite in the 3.30 at Wolverhampton. Remember, banks are only looking for a reason to refuse credit these days so keep your accounts, especially your current account, as clean as possible. A lack of credit can be a very serious situation and should be treated as such. Some bookmakers allow cash deposits in their branches but there's no real way to do this with the exchanges. There are other options for lodging money apart from direct bank transfer such as PayPal. There may be extra costs involved but it might be worth lodging money into one of these accounts and then transfer it to your exchange account to keep the transaction off your current account statement. That said, sometimes these transactions show up as PayPal but they also show the bookie/exchange name on the bank account reference. Perhaps you can set up an account with another bank for things like trading? Remember too that it looks worse if bookie/exchange transactions are a regular occurrence on your statement. One single transaction of €500 on your account may be missed or overlooked if it is far enough in the past but 25 lodgements of €20 over the space of a few months certainly won't be overlooked by the bank. I mentioned earlier about protecting your capital and staying in the game: bank statements are another reason why you must protect your capital once you've lodged money, you should avoid having too many gambling transactions on your statement.

BEWARE OF 'GAMBLER'S FALLACY'

A few years back, my wife and I had a light-hearted row when we were on a short weekend break away in the west of Ireland. For some reason, she likes to do the lottery whenever she is visiting a town outside of Dublin. I've no idea why she does this; in fact I've no idea why she does the lottery at all as the chances of winning compared to the odds you are getting are way out of line. Indecently, if you drive to the shop to get a ticket, you've more chance of getting into a serious car accident on your way to the shop than actually buying the winning ticket. I'm one of those people who believe that the lottery is a tax on people who are bad at maths and don't bother with it myself, but the wife thinks that the €4 she spends every week is worth it and it allows her to think big for a few moments before her dreams of a yacht and a private island are dashed again for another week. Anyway, while away in the countryside, she asked me to go to the shop and do the lottery for her. The six numbers I picked for her were 4, 8, 12, 16, 20, and 24. She took one look at the ticket and went nuts. "There's no way those set of numbers will come out Wayne. Why the hell didn't you do a quick pick?" I tried to point out to her that my particular six numbers had exactly the same chance of coming out as a computer-generated quick pick but she just wasn't buying it and sent me back down to the shop to get another ticket. She seemed to think that the quick pick numbers were more likely to come out because they were 'random' but mine were less likely to come out because they were in a sequence. But the fact is that a sequence of numbers such as 1, 2, 3, 4, 5, 6 has the same chance of coming up as any other particular set of numbers.

By the way if you do happen to buy lottery tickets, I've since realised that it's a bad idea to do 1,2,3,4,5,6. Apparently, quite a few people do these numbers and if you did manage to win the prize, you are more likely to have to share the money with others. But that's another story and I'm digressing a little here!

While the lotto example could be considered gambler's fallacy, the concept is best illustrated using a simple coin toss. When tossing a coin, there is a 50 percent chance that heads will come up and a 50 percent chance that tails will come up. If you are tossing the coin a number of times in a row, it doesn't matter what came up in the last toss; the chances of either heads or tails coming up is still 50:50. If, for example, a coin is tossed four times and four heads come up, the chances of tails coming up is not increased. It's still a fifty-fifty chance as **each toss is independent of any other**. It's amazing how many very bright people don't accept this. This is known as the *gambler's fallacy*. They feel that a win on tails is somehow 'overdue' and will often talk misguidedly about the 'law of averages' to back up their case. I'm slightly embarrassed to admit it now, but when I was a teenager, I fell for this way of thinking and even bought a book about roulette which gave out what it claimed were winning systems based on the 'law of averages'. I often flick through the book now and smile as it's crammed full of examples where the author relies on gambler's fallacy to back up his case.

The funny thing is, this book is still for sale and gets some great reviews on Amazon. The idea that the universe has some sort of 'memory' regarding how many heads came up previously is preposterous but this idea actually permeates our everyday lives. Traders need to be aware of gambler's fallacy and you must be sure to recognise it if you are basing some decisions on it. For example, take a trading strategy that has a historical strike rate of 50 percent and happens to fall upon five losing trades in a row: some people will up their stakes on the next trade as they feel that another bad trade is somehow unlikely. Others will succumb to 'reverse gambler's fallacy' and may feel that a losing trade is actually more likely as they feel they are on a 'losing run'. Even when you understand gambler's fallacy, you can still catch yourself having these thoughts from time to time.

IF IT LOOKS TOO GOOD TO BE TRUE...

Be careful too, of gamblers and traders offering their services and systems for sale through various websites. A few years ago, there was a software program doing the rounds which cost, from memory, around £100 per month. It was basically an automated trading system which would trade while you went to work or slept or whatever. The website was quite professional and it was getting some good reviews on forums and after a lot of wrangling, I managed to get myself a free trial. When I tried out the software, it did indeed make some money. After four days, my €100 starting bank was up to €111, which as you should know by now, is a very healthy return. It all looked very complicated and at the time, the Excel spreadsheet that placed the bets via the API was like a foreign language to me. I must admit that I was actually getting quite excited but I sensed there had to be a catch. I called a computer geek friend around one evening and we had a look at my betting records and the spreadsheet formulas together. It quickly became apparent that the 'system' it was using to trade was a simple loss chaser. It was made to look complicated in Excel but it was nothing new. It would simply back horses if and when they hit 1.10 in-running. This explained the long winning run at least. But if the horse actually went on to lose, the software would simply increase the stakes on the next bet to recover the loss — and then once the loss was recovered, it returned to normal betting. Of course, a number of losses at 1.10 in a row will not happen very often so I can see why this was getting good testimonials. However, for such a system to work, you need a bottomless bank. It's inevitable that you will hit a few losers in a row and wipe out your bank but by the time that happens, you and many others may have already paid the company a couple of hundred quid. Loss chasing is the oldest trick in the book (Google 'Martingale' to read more), it never works (long-term) and there is no need to pay people to eventually lose your money. It's an old phrase but it really is true that if something looks too good to be true, it probably is.

Another old scam to be aware of does not necessarily relate to trading although I've seen a variation of it in the financial trading world. Basically, a person would get a letter in the post (or an email these days) telling them to back a certain horse in a certain race. The horse would win and the person might be slightly interested. The next week, they would get a similar letter and yet again, the horse would win. Now the recipient becomes intrigued. The following week, the same thing; another winning tip. Depending on how determined the sender is, it may go on for about four or five weeks. The recipient of the letters would be astounded at how someone could pick five winners in a row, often at big prices. They would then get a letter saying they had to pay if they wanted the sixth tip. Again, the scam is obvious when you know how to do it but I can see why plenty of people hand over their hard-earned money to get that sixth tip. Is the tipster really that good? Does he have 'inside information' as he suggests? Unfortunately, the answer is a resounding 'no'. Some of you will be familiar with this scam already but if not, here's an example of how it works:

1. The 'tipster' selects a race with ten runners. In total, he sends out 1,000 emails. He splits the emails into ten batches of 100. In the first 100 emails, he tells the recipients to back horse number one. In the second batch, he tells them to back horse number two. In the third batch, he tells them to back horse number three and so on.

2. Horse number six wins the race. 900 people will have received a

losing tip so they are discarded — but the batch of 100 people that were told to back number six will believe he tipped a winner.

3. Next, he picks a five runner race. He sub-divides the winning 100 email address into batches of twenty. He tells the first batch of twenty to back horse number one, the second batch to back horse number two and so on.

4. Horse number one wins. 80 people will have received a losing tip but 20 will have received a winning tip (which is their second winning tip in a row).

5. He picks a four runner race. He sub-divides the winning 20 email addresses into batches of five. He tells the first batch of five to back horse number one, the second batch to back horse number two and so on.

6. Horse number three wins. 15 people will have received a losing tip but five will have had the winner. This is the third winning tip in a row that they have received.

7. He tells them that to get the fourth tip, they need to pay him money. By this stage, some will have fallen hook, line and sinker for the scam. They may even get some friends involved and club together to pay for the next tip. The 'tipster' will then select a horse from another race, usually the short-priced favourite. If it wins, everyone is still happy (for now) and he can charge even more for the next tip. If it loses, he walks off into the sunset with your money and is never heard from again.

As I say, just be aware of these sorts of scams. They abound in the world of financial trading where half the people are told to buy a stock and the other half are told to sell. I'm sure it won't be long before we see something similar emerge in the sports trading markets telling you a horse is going to steam or drift in price.

Beware too of genuine tipsters that have hit a run of good luck but now believe that they have the Midas touch and set up tipping websites. I've run a number of tipping sites over the years, and some have done better than others. Running these sites is not an easy game, especially when you hit a rough patch — although there does seem to be an insatiable appetite for them and there's often money to be made in setting them up. Hit a good patch, especially at the start, and you'll have any amount of people looking to sign up. Sometimes the problem though, is not so much the scam artists out there — it's the genuine guys who are on a winning streak and think they've cracked it. Again, take an example of a coin toss. Could you get ten in a row? You have about one chance in 1,024, according to the man who runs the Internet. So it's not impossible then, even though it is unlikely. And the more people that try, the more that will get it. If 10,000 people try it, we may get a few tens in a row. How about if 100,000 people tried it? The point is, the more people that try it, the more chance we will have of one of those people getting a long winning sequence.

Transfer this logic to the thousands of horseracing tipping sites that have popped up over the years; it's really no different. Because so many have set up, some are bound to have great winning sequences from time to time. Most tipping websites fail and disappear — but if a tipster has had ten winners in a row, he'll get plenty of attention (while we conveniently ignore all those that failed to get ten in a row). In a coin toss, it's plain to see as it is just simple sums but in racing, the tipster himself may believe he has superior form study skills. He may start charging for his services and then find it all goes downhill. But he may have made some money from subscriptions along the way.

Don't get me wrong; I'm not saying that there are no good tipsters out there — I know quite a few that make it pay — but if you are considering following one who is on a winning streak, remember to ask yourself whether it might be simply large numbers at play — because the tipster himself may not be considering that option. People like to follow 'in form' tipsters but always check their historical strike rate as regression to the mean is likely. There are tipping sites for all sorts of activities now including sports trading and my advice is to think long and hard before parting with any money. As

I said earlier, if it looks too good to be true, it probably is.

Of course, this same logic should also apply to your own trading. If you hit ten or twenty winning trades in a row, does it mean you've cracked it? If you are doing thousands of trades per year with a strategy which has a high strike rate, it's bound to happen some time. Don't get over-excited by winning sequences unless they are really out of the ordinary. Likewise, don't get too upset by losing sequences unless they too are out of the ordinary. If you know your general strike rate, you should be able to work out what sort of winning and losing sequences are likely from time to time.

RECORDS, RECORDS, RECORDS

This is one I can't stress enough. Keeping good records of your trades is imperative if you want to see where you are making and losing money. It's all too easy to forget the bad trades when a good run comes along and we start to believe we don't need to bother taking the time to write anything down. Recording your trades is, frankly, boring. But it's sobering too. How many of us have chased a loss or done a silly bet and then justified it to ourselves quickly in our brain? It's amazing how fast the brain works, and excuses in all walks of life will be formed to justify our bad behaviour. It's quite natural actually; the brain wants to put our mind and body at ease and by justifying our wrongdoing, we can somehow (in our own heads at least), make everything right in the world. For more on justifying bad decisions, have a read of the excellent book *Mistakes Were Made (But Not by Me): Why We Justify Foolish Beliefs, Bad Decisions, and Hurtful Acts* by Carol Tavris and Elliot Aronson.

It's much harder to overlook your bad decisions if you have to write down what happened. And I'm not just talking about printing off your Betfair P&L either, I'm talking about having a notepad alongside your computer and jotting down some characteristics about each trade, both good and bad. All this information can then be fed into an Excel spreadsheet after racing ends or before racing starts the following morning. Did anything unusual happen? How many runners were in the race? On a scale of ten, how volatile was the market? Did you move your stop-loss when the trade went wrong and if so, why the heck are you acting so recklessly? Were there big traders in the market? Any spoofers? What sort of volume was matched on the event? Did you go inplay without a plan and if so, why were you reckless? Was your loss on the trade more than you had anticipated before you began and if so, why?

You get the picture: forcing yourself to justify your actions can be hard to do but it's a worthwhile exercise and it helps you stay disciplined. As I say, record keeping can be boring but if you are sticking to your strategy, it won't be too cumbersome as you won't have to justify unusual or reckless behaviour. I have a template set up and printed off with about ten boxes to fill in when I first look at any market (prices, volatility, runners etc) and to be honest, it only takes less than a minute to fill out. Keep a section for 'notes' and write down anything unusual, including your own mistakes and the moments where you let your discipline slide. Each morning, I update a spreadsheet with the information from the previous day and if the 'notes' column on my spreadsheet is getting particularly busy, I get worried as it means I'm probably letting my discipline slip. Most trades should be simple and require very little note taking — you get in and then you either make a profit, or you get out. It only gets complicated when you bend the rules.

In time, your spreadsheet will build and this data can prove immensely useful. For example, I found over time that I was losing quite a bit of money trading odds-on priced horses. This was going on for some time but I simply didn't realise. When I checked back over my spreadsheet one evening, I was able to see that this was an area where I struggled. Obviously, the sample size has to be significant if you are to draw any meaningful conclusions — five or ten trades is not enough. This is why you must record every trade. I haven't cut out trading on such horses completely but I have changed my methods of trading them with some improvement. Also, when I open a market and see an odds-on horse, I immediately reduce my stakes. I'll keep the stakes to a minimum until I can see (from my good records!) that I can make these trades pay using other strategies. If I can't make it pay over time, I'll consider dropping odds-on horses completely. Cutting out certain aspects of your trading may be the difference between going from a losing trader or breakeven trader to a winning one.

Because trading is a solitary profession, it's sometimes hard to see it as a 'proper' business but if you don't treat it like a real business with yourself as the entrepreneur, it will never be a success. Yes, records are boring but, as any businessman will tell you, it's not all about fireworks and fun. Think of any successful business in your town. It may be a large chainstore or it may be the local hairdresser, restaurant or pub. Now, imagine if that business didn't bother keeping daily records of where they are spending their cash. Imagine if they simply took money in and out of the till, bought stock without getting a receipt and never sat down to do their weekly profit and loss. Would it still be a successful business? What makes you think you are any different in your trading business?

A couple of years back, I did a diploma in financial trading. We were training in a trading room environment and we all had to fill out a paper slip each time we made a trade. It was reminiscent of the old pre-computer trading pits where each trade had to be recorded manually. The type of trade made and the stakes etc. were all recorded but more importantly, we had to write down why we entered the trade and why we exited. At first, most of the class groaned at the idea and we thought it was a waste of time as our trading accounts would record everything we did electronically anyway. But what an eye-opener it turned out to be. Not only did it slow us down (our tutor reasoned that if we don't have time to fill out a slip after each trade, we are definitely taking things too fast and almost certainly over-trading), it also made us justify the times when we broke our rules or moved our stop-losses. When you have to explain your reasons for breaking the rules in front of the class, you begin to see that it's really best not to do it and by the end of the week, we had become far more disciplined. Our tutor had no problem when we reported a losing trade as long as we had stuck to our rules and not moved our stop-losses. By the end of the week, we were doing far less trading than at the start but the trades we were doing were quality trades. While it's important to turn your money over as much as you can, don't let quantity become more important than quality.

CHOOSING YOUR MARKETS

People often ask me what the best markets for trading are but that's impossible to answer as we all have different levels of risk, different times in which we can trade and of course, different sports that we understand.

A successful punter I know from Ireland makes most of his money from cricket, which might not seem unusual to British readers of this book but cricket does not enjoy a large following in Ireland so it's quite a novel way to make a living over here. I can't quite get my head around the sport and am probably best concentrating on sports I know inside out. Equally too, I like to trade the GAA sports of Gaelic Football and hurling. These are uniquely Irish sports and despite the fact that you regularly get over 80,000 people attending a match, they are not widely followed outside of Ireland. Perhaps the reason I can trade GAA sports is because I played them as a kid, can read a game, and know about each team but I reckon it would be very difficult for anyone outside Ireland to trade these. Golf is another one where money can be made but I'm just not really interested and despite trying hard to get into it, I find myself getting a little bored watching it. Golf fans may be horrified to read that but it's just the way it is and I probably don't know enough about the sport to fully appreciate it. Similarly, I know a guy who makes a decent second income trading tennis and more power to him but somehow I just can't make it click. Most people I know enjoy soccer and I've often made some money trading it — but the big games on Saturday afternoons have always clashed with racing and I can't give it my full attention.

I don't mean to sit on the fence and dodge the question of which sports are best for trading but as pointed out, different things work for different people. Whatever sport you trade, I think it's very important to have a good grasp of the rules. Personally, I like to trade horseracing and that's why most of the examples in this book come from that sport. I can only speak about what I know but I'm confident that some of the strategies within this book could be applied to other sports. After all, it's really just supply and demand and as long as you understand the rules and peculiarities of a given sport, you should be able to adapt some strategies accordingly. Indeed, I often read books about financial trading and have found that many of the same principles apply. Markets are markets and behind them all are people driving the prices.

If you are a horseracing trader, you may well ask which markets are best for making money but again, this is impossible for me to answer as I don't know your personality. Are you a swing trader who doesn't mind lots of small losses while waiting for a big win? Are you a scalper who likes lots and lots of small victories and accepts the occasional large loss? Do you like fast-paced markets which can be exciting but stressful? Do you like slow steady markets which can be rewarding but only after a long wait? As I say, everyone is different and will prefer different types of markets so I can't really say what will suit you. But what I can say, from years of watching the markets, is that you can give a good guess of how volatile a market may be before you begin trading and then make a decision to get involved or sit it out, depending on your style.

I mentioned volatility in an earlier chapter but it's worth coming back to it again. I can't back the following up with any hard evidence and it's really only my own observations — but generally speaking, I've found that **markets with plenty of liquidity (mostly high-quality races) are far steadier** than those poor quality races where a few grand could move the market. Races with **small fields tend to be quite volatile** as when a certain horse is backed, the other prices must move too in order to even out the book. In a big field, the effect of these price moves is spread amongst a lot of horses so it's not as pronounced but in a small field, prices jump or fall quite quickly. Large fields are not always steady though **and if the favourite is a short price in a large field, it could prove volatile**. Conversely, **a large field with a fairly weak favourite shouldn't throw up too many crazy price moves.**

Again, I must emphasise that this is all very general and can't be taken as Gospel. Markets change over the years, but if you spend enough time at it and keep good notes, you should eventually have that 'gut' feeling about how volatile or otherwise a market is going to be. By the way, if you are interested in the topic of gut feelings and whether they can be trusted, have a read of the extremely interesting *Thinking, Fast and Slow* by Daniel Kahneman, which explains it all much better than I could ever do. When starting out, you should only trade the favourite or second favourite as that's where the most liquidity is. Bigger-priced selections can be more volatile and trickier to trade. Even today, I rarely look outside the top two in the betting when trading on horses.

COMMISSION

I won't say too much about commission — anyone who visits the betting exchange forums will probably have had their fill already down the years. It's a pain in the arse paying commission on winnings, there's no doubt about it — and you often hear people moan about how unfair it all is. But the exchanges are not a charity and they are entitled to make money. For those of us who remember the bad old days of paying up to 10% tax on bets (and that's before the bookie over-round), a charge of up to 5% on a winning bet doesn't seem so bad, especially as the over-round on the exchanges is usually quite low. Having said all that, the premium charges for its most successful punters leaves Betfair open to criticism and they can no longer make the claim, as they used to, that they welcome winners. The other exchanges typically charge less and don't have a premium charge but liquidity, up to the time of writing, is still a problem on the other exchanges on less high-profile events. It's getting better though and most serious gamblers and traders I know have accounts with more than one exchange.

Commission does eat away at profits though, and it must be factored in. A few years ago, a mate of mine had a backing system which was losing a small amount of money (but not too much). He became frustrated but then came up with the novel idea of turning it into a lay system instead. Yet he still lost money — he hadn't factored in the cost of commission into his forecasts. A silly mistake you might think but it's quite common and you regularly hear people say things like such-and-such a team is even money on Betfair (if it is trading at 2.0). You even hear this on TV, even though the bet, if it wins, will only pay out 95p to a £1 stake if the person is on the maximum 5% commission.

As a simple example, let's say you had a series of ten bets at 2.0 on the exchanges and five of them win and five of them lose. The absolute novice might assume that the series of bets broke even. But the total loss, of course is 25p to a £1 level stake:

Losses: 5 x £1 = £5
Wins: 5 x £0.95 = £4.75

If, like my friend, you thought you could turn that into a successful lay system, you'd be wrong. The five successful lays would pay £4.75 while the five unsuccessful lays would cost £5. I know this is fairly basic stuff but otherwise intelligent people really do forget about, or ignore commission when they are working out their strategy and with margins so tight in this game, you have to account for every penny.

This applies to paper traders too and that's why it's probably best to use a small real bank when learning. When trading, I always select the option to 'display profit and loss net of commission' on my software. This way, if it says I'm going to make a tenner on a trade, I'm going to make a tenner and not a smaller amount.

STAKING

As a general rule, I never risk more than 3% of my bank on any given trade. So if my bank was £1,000, the highest amount of risk on each trade would be £30. That's risk, by the way, and not stake. For the most part though, I usually only risk between 1% and 2% of my bank. Of course, as your bank grows, you can reduce the risk (percentage wise) but allow the stakes to remain at a decent size.

Say, for example, you have a bank of £1,000 and are risking 2% per trade which is £20. And assume your trading is going very well and your bank eventually doubles to £2,000. You could then drop the risk on each trade to 1% (which protects your capital) but the amount of risk per trade is still £20. That said, it's important to use your money too and there's no point in having, say, ten grand sitting in Betfair doing nothing if you are only using a couple of hundred of it. In that case, a big lump sum would be better off sitting in a high-interest deposit account. But as I say, using a small percentage of your bank on each trade is a useful way to go and, in theory at least, will make it very difficult to bust your bank.

Of course, if you are using the same stake on each trade, your risk and reward will be different depending on the prices so it's best to move away from that practice and trade in 'tick sizes' instead. After all, **having £100 on something priced 7.6 which moves two ticks is a hell of a lot different than having £100 on something priced 1.6 which moves two ticks**. This is an extremely important point which sometimes gets overlooked. So what we need to do is adjust the stake in relation to the price. It's easier to control risk if each move represents the same loss or gain no matter what the price. Let's say you want to trade in ticks of £1: that is, for every price movement, you will win or lose £1 (before you green/red up the book). To trade in a £1 tick size, you must adjust your stakes as follows:

From 1.01 to 2.0, use a stake of £100
From 2.02 to 3.0, use a stake of £50
From 3.05 to 4.0, use a stake of £20
From 4.10 to 6.0, use a stake of £10
From 6.2 to 10.0, use a stake of £5
From 10.5 to 20.0, use a stake of £2

You can work out the higher prices for yourself if you wish but I don't recommend you trade in those ranges as the market is usually illiquid and unpredictable on the bigger-priced selections.

Some programs will help you out with tick size trading; on Bet Angel for example, you can simply type in the tick size you wish to trade in and it will automatically use the right sized stake depending on the prices, which is quite handy.

STOP-LOSSES

I've mentioned stop-losses various times throughout this book but you may have noticed that I don't have any hard and fast rules about where to place them. I'm often asked about stops and while I do think they are essential (to take out the difficult human element of cutting your losses), it's like asking how long is a piece of string because each market has its own nuances. For example, I could advise you to use a stop-loss of four pips in a given strategy but what if the four pips stop-loss happens to fall on a major area of resistance? Or what if it is at a crossover price? Generally speaking, you should keep your stops tight for swing trading (which involves lots of small losses and one or two big wins) and a little bit looser for scalping (which involves lots of small wins and the odd big loss). It's like playing poker — as

Kenny Rogers sang, you have to *know when to hold 'em and know when to fold 'em*. A good poker player doesn't expect to win every hand. Folding in poker is like having a stop-loss in trading. There may be some false starts and you may have to fold a number of times before you play along — but when your cards come good, the rewards will be waiting and all the small losses can be recovered. As a general rule, I decide in advance how much I'm willing to lose on each trade and then set my stops accordingly. If, therefore, you want to use wide stops, you will have to reduce your stakes.

I know one or two traders who use mental stops (they don't actually place stop-losses but they get out when the market goes against them) and I respect their discipline. Personally, I still find it hard to pull the trigger and get out of a trade when it goes wrong so in some strategies, I still need to set automatic stops. Once a stop is set, I adjust it if necessary to move it away from crossover prices etc. but that's about it. Once it's in place in your desired spot, leave it there.

When you decide on a stop-loss before you enter a trade, you are doing so rationally and with a clear state of mind. Once we are in a trade, we don't think as clearly as we are emotionally involved with the position. That's why I think it's often a bad idea to place stop-losses after a trade has been opened. If you find that you are moving stops further away as soon as it becomes clear you are going to hit it, then you are not acting rationally. You have let emotion take you over. We've all been there and I've done it myself. You make excuses as to why the stop-loss is in the wrong place or why 'it's different this time'. Once you start making these excuses and moving your stops, you've lost the plot. You originally set the stop in a rational state of mind so what has changed now that you're actually close to hitting it? Emotion, fear and greed — that's what.

A few weeks ago, I was at the circus with my daughter and she watched in delight as the trapeze artist swung high in the air, hanging off the swing with her legs. But the trapeze artist wasn't a fool — she had a safety net in place as she knew the trick could sometimes go wrong. Stop-losses are your safety net. It's never nice when things go wrong and the safety net is called into action — but at least it saves your bacon and allows you to live to fight another day.

Most traders will have heard the phrase 'cut your losses and let your profits run' but in actual fact, most of us do the opposite. We let our losing trades run and run and run but as soon as we see some profit, we take it too early. Why is it so hard to cut losses? I guess that crystallising a loss and making it real can be tricky. If we hold on to it, there's always the possibility that it will turn around but if we exit our trade for a loss then we have to accept that we got it wrong which, as mentioned numerous times, is easier said than done. But bad trades that are let run are like bad fruit — they spread their misery all around. If you ran a fruit and vegetable shop, you wouldn't keep the bad apples in with the good ones in the hope that someone will come along and buy them. You would simply chuck them out and accept a small loss on each, knowing that the profit from the good apples will ensure you make a profit on the box of apples overall. Leaving them there to rot would turn the good ones sour. It's the same with your losing trades. If you don't cut your losses and chuck out your bad trades, they will eat away at your bank, leaving you less to trade with. That means your good trades won't produce as much profit. You know the lesson here: chuck out your bad apples and protect your bank.

As humans, we have an in-built tendency to get attached to things we've bought or received. Even if these things turn out to be bad (like a losing trade), we still find it hard to let them go. Have you ever rented a movie or bought a book that you didn't like but stuck with it nonetheless? This is known as the 'sunk cost' effect whereby we continue (often unwisely) with our purchase as we have already invested our time or money in it and don't want to let that time or money 'go to waste'. Similarly, we also justify expensive purchases to ourselves, even if everyone else can see that we wasted our money. In fact, once we come to own anything (including a trade) it becomes surprisingly hard to give it up.

In the international bestseller mentioned earlier *Thinking Fast And Slow*, author Daniel Kahneman discusses an experiment whereby two classes were asked to fill out a questionnaire. Each class was rewarded with a gift for doing so. The gift they received had remained in front of them while they filled out the questionnaire:

'In one session, the prize was an expensive pen; in another, a bar of Swiss chocolate. At the end of the class, the experimenter showed the alternative gift and allowed everyone to trade his or her gift for another. Only 10% of the participants opted to exchange their gift. Most of those who had received the pen stayed with the pen, and those who had received the chocolate did not budge either.'

The point is that once we own something (including a trade), we get attached to it, even if it is going wrong. Simply being aware of this fact in both trading and in general life might help you cut losses a little easier. As mentioned before, you should be of the view that anything can happen in a market and you must be prepared for all possibilities. Remember: amateurs enter trades, hope for the best and exit on the spur of the moment. Professionals **spend as much time on their exit point as they do on their entry point.**

TAKING OUT THE STOPS

That's not to say that stop-losses are not problematic in themselves. As always, there are people out there on the exchanges trying to second guess what you are doing and will try to make money accordingly. One of the main issues with stops, especially if you are doing something like support and resistance trading (see chapter seven), is that most people will place their stop-losses in the same sort of places. If you do this, it can leave you vulnerable. I'm guilty of this myself and often get caught out. Take, for example, the following scenario:

- The price of a certain selection has been trading between 6.4 and 7.0 for quite some time.
- The price has risen to 7.0 numerous times but never broke through the ceiling.
- The price has also tested the 6.4 floor price a number of times without breaking through.
- As you get ready to trade, the price is at 6.6 and heading north again on strong volume.

What do you do right now? Most people would probably lay the selection while it's heading north — and then back it when it hits the ceiling price. What about the stop-loss? Have a think for a moment about where you'd place your stop if you had layed at 6.6.

The obvious place is just under the floor at 6.2 right? After all, the price has tested 6.4 (the floor) a number of times already and is unlikely to break through again. If you agreed with 6.2, which I assume most readers have, therein lies the problem with stop-losses. If 6.2 seems an obvious place to put the stop-loss to you and me, it's also obvious to another trader looking to take our money. How can another trader exploit us if they know where our stops are? Well, if they have a big enough bank, they can back the price all the way down to 6.2. If this happens, your stop will be hit and you take a loss. Yes, the other trader takes a risk that the price will continue to fall — but if the market is at least somewhat efficient, other value-seeking layers will step back in at this point and bring the price back up to its 'proper' price of between 6.4 and 7.0.

Boom! You've just been taken out. As the price returns to its natural level, the other crafty trader hitches a ride along the way and then cashes out for a profit. In the meantime, you are left to stare at a red screen.

What can one do to avoid getting taken out? It's hard to say really and sometimes we just have to take a risk and hope it doesn't happen. It's an occupational hazard and it happens to us all. In a case like this, you could consider taking some extra risk and placing your stop at 6.0 or even further below at 5.8. Because 6.0 is a crossover price (see chapter four), it will take a lot of money to smash through it so your stop should be safe enough at 5.8. But the downside, of course, is an extra-big loss when it does go wrong (which it will from time to time).

Most of us don't have a big enough bank to push the market around like the trader(s) that took us out but I've been working on a strategy lately which operates on a similar principle and tries to piggyback what those guys do:

Again, we will use the same example:

- The price of a certain selection has been trading between 6.4 and 7.0 for quite some time.

- The price has risen to 7.0 numerous times but never broke through the ceiling.
- The price has also tested the 6.4 floor price a number of times without breaking through.
- As you get ready to trade, the price is at 6.6 and heading north again on strong volume.

Instead of backing the selection at 6.6 and trying to trade out at a higher price, you could consider putting in a lay order at 6.2. As mentioned, there will be a lot of stop-losses at this price and other big traders know this. Next, you simply wait until the big traders push the price down to hit the stops at 6.2. A lot of the time, you will be left waiting and no trade will occur. But that's fine, we don't lose money by not trading. If the big traders do push the price down to the stops at 6.2, your lay bet gets hit and your trade is open. Then, you wait for market efficiency to kick in and bring the price back to its natural level between 6.4 and 7.0. When it reaches that level, you place your back bet and exit your trade for a profit. Your stop-loss, in this case, could be set at 5.8 as you have the added protection of the crossover price of 6.0 (which will be hard to break through) up over you.

REDDENING THE BOOK

When we get a successful trade, we rarely let the bet stand on the single selection; most of us will 'green up' the book and spread the profit around to ensure a good result no matter what the outcome of the event. But what about when a trade goes wrong and you are stopped out for a loss? Should you turn the whole book red or should you take a chance and hope the loss is not materialised? If you red up the book, you are ensuring a small loss no matter what selection wins the event whereas if you simply leave one selection red and the others at zero, you will only lose money if that selection wins the event. But if you chose the latter option, the losses will be big when they eventually come around. It's a tricky one; logic says that if you green up the book on a successful trade, you should go red when things don't go your way. But studies have shown that we are more inclined to gamble when facing the choice between a certain loss and a possible neutral outcome and that tendency often reveals itself when trading. The most sensible thing to do is to turn the book red but I must admit that I often deviate from that rule myself, depending on the price of the selection. If we take the odds as a fair reflection of its chances, then it would make sense to spread the loss of a horse for example, which is priced 1.2 (as its chance of winning is supposedly over 83%). But if the horse is priced 5.0, it only has a 20% chance of winning so I may decide to take a chance and let the bet stand. I do realise though, that letting the bet stand is gambling and should probably be avoided. It's something I'm working on but I allow myself to break the rules the odd time. If, for example, I have had a very successful day and don't want to end it on a low, I will take a chance and hope the red selection doesn't win. Psychologically, that lets me end on a high but when it goes wrong, it's a kick in the teeth and can undo half a day of work sometimes. It's personal preference really but most successful traders I've spoken to would recommend that you make the book go red. As mentioned before, it's not ideal to think of trading in terms of hours or days as it's supposed to be a long-term ongoing process.

NO-ONE'S PERFECT

The problem with many traders is that they are looking for the perfect system or set-up that will consistently make them money without fail. But there is no perfect system or set-up out there; we have to make do with some good ones instead. We need to accept that our systems are not perfect and don't always go to plan. Outside the world of betting and trading, we have many systems in our lives and not all go to plan either. You set your alarm every morning at the same time, get a shower and breakfast, and leave your house just in time to catch your train to work. For the most part, this systematic approach to your morning works for you and 99 times out of 100 you arrive at work on time. It's effective but it's not perfect. What would happen if the train you were on broke down? You could try to accommodate that possibility by getting an earlier train just in case, thereby sacrificing some sleep. But what if a pipe burst when you turned on your shower? Again, this would cause delays. You could try getting up even earlier just in case that happens too. But what if...

The point I'm making here is that no system in our life is perfect. If you were to try to consider every possibility when planning your journey to work every day, you simply wouldn't get any sleep. You have to accept the inconvenient fact that unusual things happen from time to time. This doesn't mean our 'system' for getting ourselves to work isn't effective. Generally speaking, it's very good — but it's not perfect. When creating betting or trading systems, people often try to accommodate for every possibility. Perfectly good money-making systems are destroyed in the quest for perfection. People come up with all sorts of complicated set-ups and scenarios that try to cover every angle but in the end they end up losing more money than they would have had they not started tinkering. Accept that things will go wrong from time to time when trading and remember that the simple set-ups are usually the best.

A DAY IN THE LIFE

Friday, 16th June 2012

Back in 2006, British band The Streets released an album entitled *The Hardest Way to Make an Easy Living*. It's not generally my kind of music but it was a good album nonetheless. The title of that album reminds me of trading; most people think it's an easy life just clicking away on the computer and letting the money roll in. But trading is actually one of the hardest jobs of all — and when I describe a typical day to friends and family, they are often quite surprised by the amount of work I actually do. There's plenty of times when I get up at six in the morning and work right on past midnight, only stopping for a few breaks throughout the day. Summertime is my busiest period with racing on both during the day and the evening and very often, you'll have some other major sporting events on too. To give the reader a flavour of what a typical day in the life of a trader might involve, I decided to chronicle a single day; Friday, 16th June 2012. It's a couple of years ago now but it was a good example of a busy day with lots of sport and other activities going on. No two days are the same, of course, and every week that passes throws up plenty of surprises. But the following log would be fairly typical of how I'd spend my Friday, which is generally my busiest day of the week. I'm no philosopher but hope readers will find some simple bits of advice on trading and also some advice for life in general. That particular day was quite full and I've included my non-trading activities too to illustrate how I try my best to get the balance right between work/family/fitness etc. The purpose here is to give you an idea how much work is involved in a full day.

6.00 a.m.

The alarm goes off and it's time for another day. About a year ago, I got into the habit of getting up this early. People often claim that they don't have enough hours in the day but yet they will lie in bed until the last possible minute, resetting the alarm clock every ten minutes. I only need six hours sleep per night so if I'm in bed for midnight, I usually don't have a problem getting up. As Bill Cullen (from the Irish *Apprentice* TV show) once said, "sleeping is the closest you can get to being dead; so don't do too much of it". Indeed, you'll be dead for long enough so you've got to make the most of your waking hours while you have the chance. It took about a month or two to get into the habit of getting up early but now it is second nature. When trying to get into this habit, each morning I would simply set my alarm clock ten minutes earlier than the previous morning so making the adjustment wasn't such a great shock to the system. I find that the two hour period from 6 a.m. until 8 a.m. is a great time to catch up on work and get stuff done while the house is quiet and most people are still snoozing in bed.

6.15 a.m.

I go to the kitchen and make a fruit drink in the blender. While I've never been overweight, for a while I was getting lazy and eating unhealthy food. So about six months ago, I made a conscious decision to get more fruit and veg every day. Eating the wrong foods can make you sluggish; especially if you are sitting at a computer all day. Years spent sitting at a computer eating rubbish snacks throughout the day can have a detrimental effect on your health and store up problems for later in life so it's important to me that I take control of this area. Being honest, I'm not crazy about vegetables so getting my five a day can be a bit of a chore — but it's important to look to the future and I've now made it a habit. Blending them up in a drink is an easy way to do it and you can just knock it back, even if it doesn't taste great. I like most fruits though so I don't mind having that in the morning. I'm not a healthy food freak or anything; I still enjoy the odd bit of fast food once a week but I don't feel too guilty if I've had my five a day. Speaking of snacking at the desk, raisins and different types of nuts are healthy and sometimes stop me from eating rubbish. Prunes too, have lots of antioxidants although they are not a particular favourite of mine. I turn my computers on and make a list of things I want to get done today. It's important to make a list and prioritise what I want to get done.

6.30 a.m.

I open up my spread trading platform and check what the financial markets have been up to in the overnight Asian trading. I'm bearish on the Euro in the medium-term but these markets are very tricky to trade right now. Two news items dominate the markets and it's hard to see which way the market will go: Spain's bond yields have gone above seven percent (which is generally considered close to bailout land) and Greece is facing another election this weekend. I'm tempted to try to scalp a few quid on the choppy markets but deep down I know it would be out-and-out gambling without any real strategy. I decide to close down my financial screens and park it for another day; there's no point in trading just for the sake of some action.

6.45 a.m.

With no financial trading opportunities, it's time to go back to the sports markets. There's plenty of racing on later today and also some Euro 2012 football. Firstly, I feed in yesterday's data from my handwritten notes to Excel. I then get to work looking for horses for my inplay trading strategy (see chapter fifteen) and find six potential candidates. It's now a matter of watching their previous races and going through their formbook comments to make sure I'm happy that they are likely to trade at a lower price in-running than their Betfair SP. This is quite time-consuming and sometimes I'm tempted to skip over it — but I remind myself that hard work is the only way to make this game pay and there is no such thing as a free lunch. I spend a couple of hours on this and eventually end up with three horses to trade. I'm not sure if I'll be at the computer for these races, so I set up Gruss Software to place the trades automatically on an old spare computer I have. I then get my daughter's breakfast ready while she prepares to go to school.

8.45 a.m.

I walk my daughter to school which only takes a few minutes. The school is literally down the road from our house so I'm very lucky in that respect. While walking home, an idea pops into my head about trading. I **always** carry a small notebook and pen around with me to write down ideas when I'm out and about. The notebook is not just for trading ideas; it's for all walks of life and I'd encourage every reader to do this. Reminding yourself to follow something up by writing it down will ensure it will get done. If you don't write it down, you will most likely forget. You never know when a good (possibly money-making) idea will pop into your head and it's amazing how many times I take out the notebook each week and scribble something down for following up later. Getting tasks done and crossed off the list has made me much more organised and successful in many areas of my life. At first, I used to make these notes on my iPhone but even though I love technology, I find that the simple pen and paper is much handier and quicker.

9.00 a.m.

I head out for a 5K run. I like to run 3-4 times per week and it's something I enjoy immensely. Paradoxically, the more exercise you do the more energy you have throughout the day. Before I got into running, I would feel tired and sluggish sitting at the computer screen throughout the day and my mental alertness wasn't what it should have been. By the time the evening trading session would come around, I would be slumped in the chair, jaded and tired, even though I hadn't moved much all day. A run is a great way to start the day and it also keeps me fit. I've decided to run my first marathon (26.2 miles) in Dublin in October so I'm trying to do a bit more running each week to build up my fitness. When I was in my 20s, keeping fit and healthy wasn't on my list of priorities but now that I'm in my 30s, it has become very important. There's no point in working hard at trading for a couple of decades only to find that you are plagued with ill-health later in life. I've seen a number of financial traders wear themselves out physically and emotionally and if you don't make time to keep fit and well, it's all pointless as you won't be able to enjoy the fruits of your labour. Running is also a great way to clear the head and get away from stress. Feel-good endorphins are released and a good exercise workout is now becoming recognised as something that can help those with depression too. When I stick the iPod on and get running, all the cares of the world disappear for a time and it's a chance to get away from it all, including trading. People often complain that they don't have time to go do some exercise but you have to make time. I know how it feels to come home from work and slump down in front of the TV completely shattered but I can assure you that once you are exercising on a regular basis, the lack of energy won't be as profound. Start off gradually and add a few minutes extra each week. I hate to lecture but I dislike it when people give me the excuse that they can't find the time. If you are not arsed, just admit that — but also accept the consequences. Can you cut out 15 minutes of television each day? That's 105 minutes per week straight off. Can you get up an hour earlier each morning? Another 420 minutes to play around with. Can you spend a half hour less down the pub each week? You get the picture. Every one of us is given 168 hours each week. If you sleep for seven hours per night that leaves 119 waking hours. Assuming you work a 40 hour week, you are still left with 79. Surely you can fit in 2-3 hours of exercise in there somewhere? After my run, I have a quick shower and a small bite to eat before I get back to work.

10.00 a.m.

It's quite a hectic day for sport, there's racing on from Aintree, Chepstow, Clonmel, Goodwood, Musselburgh, Navan, Sandown and York. Later on in the football, England take on Sweden in the European Championships. It's going to be a busy day. I've to write an article for Saturday's *Irish Independent* newspaper too which will take up half of the day, so I'll have to pick and choose what events I'm going to trade. Musselburgh, Sandown and York are daytime meetings so I scratch them from the list to concentrate on my writing. I've learned the hard way that you can't do two things at once when trading; you have to give it your full attention. The newspaper copy must be in by 3.30 p.m. so that's where I must focus my attention for the next few hours. It's basically a tipping piece and the word count is 800-1000 words, depending on space. Luckily enough, I already have some ideas to write about and have been working on some stuff throughout the week. Sports journalism is not as easy as it might appear and a lot of background work goes into each article. Even though the article gets written on the Friday, I actually spend quite a bit of time throughout the week doing some research, checking the stats, looking for good bets and ringing around contacts in the industry fishing for news and prices. It's something I enjoy immensely however, and I'd like to do even more of it in the future.

12.30 p.m.

Lunch. I'm not too hungry today so I just have something small. Even if I'm not hungry, I still take a break away from the computer. I'll often go for a short walk to clear the head or else ring a mate or my wife for a quick chat. It's important to make contact with the outside world — many traders don't do much of it.

1.00 p.m.

I begin work again on tomorrow's newspaper article. By 2 p.m. I'm almost done but then I notice a story on the *Racing Post* website stating that one of my tips is unlikely to run due to the ground. I'm now under strong pressure to re-write some of my copy but I get it done and file it with my editor at 3.25 p.m. Just like trading, you must always be prepared for unusual circumstances and be able to react quickly. It can be especially tricky in the wintertime when you may have spent the whole morning writing about an upcoming meeting only for it to be abandoned due to the weather. The summertime flat racing is a lot less stressful. Once I hit the send button, there's no going back or hiding — my tips will be printed in black and white in the morning. You've got to be thick-skinned in this business. You will rarely be praised for a winner but you sure as hell will get slated for a string of losers. My column is showing a reasonable profit for the year overall which is pleasing — although my conscience often plays at me if I have a bad day. I sometimes wonder if someone followed my advice and went home to his missus empty-handed after a day at the bookies. At the end of the day though, every adult must make (and take responsibility for) their own decisions. I still get a kick out of seeing my name in print in newspapers. As my late uncle Dave (who lived a very colourful life) used to say, "It's good to see the Bailey name printed in the paper — outside of the court pages this time!"

3.30 p.m.

I've already missed a good deal of racing and trading but it can't be helped as I had other work to do. I'm quite tempted to trade a few races from the daytime meetings but I stop myself from doing so as I know that jumping in on a whim rarely pays off. Because I've been concentrating on other work, I'm not 'tuned in' to the markets. You need to pick the meetings you wish to trade, start off slowly, and get a feel for your opponent(s). I find that each day has a different mood, and tapping into that mood takes time. Jumping in now for the sake of some action would be amateurish. Amateurs give away their edge by hopping straight into the water with two feet. Professionals dip their toe a number of times before easing in slowly. At times like this, I often ask myself "what would I have done five years ago?" Five years ago, I would have tried to trade a few races — but five years ago, I was losing money. It's a no-brainer then; I close the lid of the laptop and take a couple of hours off.

The evening racing kicks off at 5.10 p.m. with Clonmel. This gives me an hour and a half to spend a bit of time with my daughter. She's seven now and I know it's an old cliché, but they grow up so fast. It's important to me that I spend some time with her every single day. I know some financial traders that have practically missed their children grow up as they just couldn't take a break from the computer in case they missed some action. I find this sad. On their death bed, if you asked them their regrets, I doubt they'll say "I wish I had spent more time in the office". My daughter and I grab the dog and take a walk down to the beach. Later, we get home and I cook some dinner. Cooking is another interest of mine. In January, I made a pact that I'd learn to cook one new dish per week. It's not a big commitment really but when you think about it, by the end of the year I will have learned how to cook 52 new things which is a pretty useful skill to have. Once fed, I turn on the TV and get the computer ready for the evening trading session.

5.00 p.m.

I'm late getting started but I'm now ready and looking forward to putting in a decent few hours of trading. As mentioned, there's no point in trying to do two things at once and both jobs will suffer as a result. I think it's critical that market participants allocate 'trading time' for themselves where they can completely absorb themselves in the markets away from distractions. If you live with family or friends, you must make it clear to them that this is your time and that you shouldn't be disturbed. Turn off the mobile phone and stay away from Facebook and the like. As usual, I ease into the markets only risking a couple of quid on each trade. After five or six races, I'm settling in nicely and decide to up the stakes. There's nothing too unusual happening although I do notice that one particular trader is putting in orders of 20 grand and then taking them back out again. It's probably someone trying to 'bully' the markets and push the prices around but I try not to let it bother me anymore and I reckon these traders are best ignored. Sometimes, you may end up on the wrong side of a price move if they do decide to actually use that money but a lot of the time, they won't actually go ahead with the order and commit the money. Other times, you might get lucky and end up on the good side of a price move but it evens out over time and I try not to get sucked into playing games against these bullies. I'm not quite sure if there's money to be made by bullying the markets. I tried a few times to do it with a couple of grand in the lightly-traded Irish horseracing markets but actually found myself getting tied up in positions which I didn't want. Maybe there's a way to make money from it but I haven't discovered it yet.

By 7.00 p.m. I'm up around fifty quid but a momentary lapse in concentration sees a trade go in-running by mistake and I have to close it out for a loss of thirty. I'm pretty annoyed with myself and should have been keeping a better eye on the clock. I realise that my sound alerts are not switched on and reactivate my software to make a beep when we hit 30 seconds before the scheduled off time. I cannot emphasise enough how important it is to avoid going in-running on horseracing (unless it is part of a pre-defined strategy). Most of my biggest losses occurred by going in-running and it is something I have stopped doing now — although I do admit that the temptation is often there when a trade has gone wrong. But the losses can be catastrophic, and whenever I'm tempted, I glance up at some screenshots I've pinned to the wall which were taken following some almighty clangers. That always brings me back to my senses. Remember; if you are still allowing your trades to go in-running and it's not part of a pre-defined strategy, you are simply gambling. It may work out for a while but it's no different to betting on black or red down at the casino. It's out and out gambling and you need to admit that to yourself. We are not supposed to be in the business of pure gambling so if you are still doing it, you need to stop. If you continue, at least accept that you are a gambler and not a trader.

Shortly before the England/Sweden Euro 2012 game, I back England with a view to laying out for a free bet should they score first. This is partly a traditional bet rather than a trade as I think England are overpriced and I fancy them to win. I don't go to town with my stakes as I'm not really an expert on football but it's just one of those hunches and I think I can make a few quid. I record the bet in my spreadsheet as a 'fun' bet. I have a completely separate bank for fun bets and always make a note of them. Your 'fun bets' money MUST be separate from your trading capital and even though they might only be for small change, it's essential that you record how much you are spending. There's nothing wrong with having a few quid on a team or horse now and again to give you a better interest in the event but recording these bets can be a real eye-opener. A fiver here watching a match in the pub, a tenner there on a dog in the bookies; it all adds up. I've cut back drastically on my fun bets in recent years as they were simply costing too much money over time. And there's nothing fun about losing money is there? Luckily, Andy Carroll gets the first midway through the first half and I lay England for the same stake I've backed them with, thus ensuring a profit if they win and no monetary loss to me if they lose. As I'm sure my English readers will remember, the match was not as easy as it appeared on paper although they eventually pulled it out of the bag and won 3-2. A small profit of fifteen quid gained overall.

At Ascot the layers are taking a hammering with six out of seven favourites winning. Fortunately, I've been concentrating on the jolly here and it's starting to pay off. There's been a decent amount of money coming for the favourite each time and as punters get more confident, they are putting their money back through the markets. Plenty of 'traditional' punter money in the markets (rather than simply trader money) is always good and there are quite a few opportunities offered to exploit due to the fact that these punters are paying less attention to detail and are not as worried as a trader would be regarding the exact price tick they get. As such, strategies like the 'key prices' and the 'magnet effect' are working a treat. I'm averaging thirty quid a race at Ascot and with seven races on the card, I'm very pleased with that result. In contrast though, Clonmel is proving difficult to trade and I've lost seventy quid trying to trade that meeting so far. Interestingly, not one favourite wins from the eight races. At Goodwood, I catch a lovely swing trade on the second favourite and as the trade goes my way, I add more cash to it — while moving my stop-loss to break even. It's a risky strategy as I could end up giving my profit back to the market but when you pull it off and the move continues in your direction, it can be lucrative.

We come to the last race of the day at 9.20 p.m. and I immediately halve my stakes. I'm not quite sure if this is a psychological thing on my part put I always find both the first and last race of the day tricky to trade. You are never quite sure what forces are at play. Will you see some big orders from people trying to recover their losses from the day? Will winners play up their money? Also known as The Great Get-out Stakes, the last race of the day often proves volatile. Many gamblers can't accept that 'tomorrow is another day' and they will play up winnings or chase losses on the closing race. I trade the favourite but once I'm in a good position, I green up and call it a day. I check my P&L and it tells me that I've made eighty-two quid. It's not a fortune but it's still over eighteen quid an hour on average for my four hour shift. When you add that to the money I'll earn from writing. It's been a productive and successful day overall.

11.00 p.m.
I close down the laptop for the day and watch a bit of TV with the missus. We've both had a busy day and didn't get to spend much time together so we agree to have a night out for a meal during the week. Again, it's important to make definite plans to spend time with your family and friends, otherwise it just gets put on the long finger. We arrange a babysitter for Wednesday. There's a news/current affairs programme I watch around this time that gives a good round-up of the day's political, financial and sporting events. Normally, I'm a bit of a news junkie but Fridays are very busy for me so I haven't had much time for TV or radio. It's important to keep up-to-date with general news and sport for both financial trading and sports trading purposes.

11.30 p.m.
I wind down the day by reading a book and having a nice glass of red wine. Every year, I do some sort of evening education course just to learn new skills

and keep the brain ticking over and in 2011, I chose to do a wine appreciation course. I'm no cork-dork and I'm certainly not aloof about which alcoholic beverages I consume but I do like to treat myself to a nice bottle and have a glass or two after a hard day. There's plenty of antioxidants in red wine and it's been proven to be good for the heart — in moderation of course.

12.00 a.m.

Bed! I set the alarm for six — Saturday is always a busy day in sport and I want to make sure I get up early enough to study the day's events. By this stage of the week, I'm getting quite tired but I always take Sunday off as a day of rest to recharge the batteries. It's been a long day but I've accomplished everything I put on my 'to do' list early this morning. Whenever I don't accomplish something on the list, it will go on tomorrow's list marked as a priority item.

CREATING A TRADING PLAN

It takes as much energy to wish as it does to plan — Former First Lady, Eleanor Roosevelt

AS mentioned before, if you want to become a successful trader, you need to treat it like a business. And no-one would start up a business without a business plan right? Yet it still amazes me how many traders want to skip over this bit. Coming up with a business plan (or trading plan as I call it) seems to be the last thing on the mind of a newbie trader — they simply want to go to battle with their account which has been freshly loaded up with money. Perhaps you too are thinking of skipping over this dull chore — after all, you're the one in charge of your account and it's not as if you will be presenting your plan to anyone. But I would absolutely urge you to give it a shot and my own trading improved no end once I had a plan in place. If you were setting out on a long journey along unfamiliar roads in your car, you'd use a map. Without a sense of direction, we simply lose track. When we don't have a firm sense of how or where our business is going, complacency creeps in. Remember; the margins are tight in trading — every penny is a prisoner in this game and there's no room for complacency. If you can improve your results even a small bit by implementing a business plan, then it's worth the effort.

Your business plan/trading plan doesn't have to be incredibly elaborate. My trading plan consists of **a few simple statements** on ten important topics. I review my plan on the first day of each month and if I'm straying away from a particular statement, I pin that statement to the wall for the month to remind myself to keep on track. Set up a reminder in your calendar to do this. You can come up with statements of your own but here's a list of ten typical questions you may like to think about and you may like to create statements based on those questions. Below that, I've discussed each topic further and have given an example statement for each. These statements are your compass and should be taken very seriously and reviewed regularly to make sure you are staying on course.

1. Why become a trader?
2. How much time can I devote to trading?
3. What strategies will I use?
4. What is a comfortable level of risk for me?
5. What kind of records am I going to keep?
6. What are my rules for when I have a winning/losing day?
7. What are my rules about withdrawing money?
8. What are the associated costs of trading and how am I going to fund them?
9. Other than money, how am I going to reward myself for all my hard work?
10. How much money or time am I willing to spend on blogging, networking and education?

1. Why become a trader?

The obvious answer to this question is, of course, money. But we need to delve a little further than that. For a start, you have to ask yourself (roughly) what sort of money you are looking to make and for what reasons. Money is an interesting concept which is built on trust. A £20 note, after all, is just a piece of paper. But that piece of paper has inherent power, as long as we all go along with the concept. As part of your trading plan, you have to examine your attitude to money and how comfortable (or otherwise) you are with earning it, saving it, betting it, spending it, investing it and sharing it. It might sound strange to say that some people are uncomfortable earning money but some psychologists believe that a lot of us have self-sabotaging tendencies when we start earning more than we subconsciously think we 'deserve'. I used to think this was nonsense until I helped mentor a trader who seemed to hit a psychological barrier every time his account went past €1,000. Overall, he was an excellent trader and managed to increase his €500 starting bank steadily right up to a grand, using some well thought-out strategies. But any time he went over €1,000, he just seemed to get nervous and would end up on a losing streak or becoming reckless. I now recognise this as a self-sabotage tendency due to his attitude towards money. He had absolutely no problem turning a €500 trading bank into

€550 in the space of a month but he could never seem to turn €1,000 into €1,100 in the same time. As strange as it sounds, he just became overwhelmed and nervous with figures above €1,000 as he believed he was no longer just 'playing around'. Here we had a perfectly good trader who, for a variety of psychological reasons, couldn't trade with large sums. He just couldn't scale up. You might think it won't happen to you but it's actually quite common.

Like me, this guy grew up in a working-class estate and he once admitted that he felt a little guilty trading with large sums of money when there were people around him that had barely any money whatsoever. Had he grown up in an affluent household, he may have had a different attitude to the value of a grand. Your upbringing has a big influence on how you view money and how you feel about earning it, spending it and risking it. For example, I was raised as a Catholic and in that community, there was always a bit of guilt associated with earning lots of money or even saving it. Being poor is almost seen as a virtue in Catholicism. Today, I certainly still believe in sharing, helping the poor and all that stuff but I think that some of the negative attitudes we were taught with regard to money were misplaced. But you don't have to have had a religious upbringing to see this type of attitude — plenty of people grew up with a similar distrust of both money and the rich. How many of us have been told that money is the root of all evil? That happens to be one of the misquoted lines from the Bible. It actually says that the *love of money* is the root of all evil. I like earning money but I'm still OK with that quote from the Bible. Because I don't love money; it's just paper. I don't particularly love paper. What I do love, however, is the freedom those pieces of paper give me. Freedom away from work and freedom from giving my precious time away. And make no mistake, your time is absolutely precious.

My attitude to earning money is quite simple: if I live to the age of 80 (which is optimistic), I will have spent 62 adult years on this earth, or just over 22,000 days. Those days are ticking away and no-one can make it stop, not even a billionaire. That thought is quite sobering and it makes me think about how I'm going to spend those hours. Stopping that clock from ticking is the one thing that money cannot buy on this earth — and that makes those hours extremely precious. What money can do, however, is allow me to decide how I wish to spend those hours.

In a week, there are 168 hours. Assuming we sleep eight hours per night (one third of that time), we are left with 112 waking hours. If you do a five-day 40-hour week, and spend two hours a day on getting ready/travelling to and from your job, that will take up 50 of those 112 hours. When you think about it like that, the amount of time we spend working (usually for other people) is actually ludicrous considering we only get one life. What can be done to 'buy' back some of those precious hours? Earning an extra income through trading is one possibility and if you are successful, you may then be able to cut back on the hours spent at your regular job. There's an old quote which says 'give a man a job he loves and he'll never work a day in his life'.

Of course you have to consider the amount of hours you will be trading and put a value on that time too. If you are earning £15 per hour in your job but are only averaging £8 per hour trading, well then we have a mismatch. Or if you are breaking even or losing at trading, then you may have to face some difficult choices. As I say, you have to ask yourself if it is worth spending your precious hours trading — and for some, it's not. But if you are averaging £30 per hour trading and £15 in your job, then that's a different story. Or perhaps you are only earning a small amount trading at the moment— but if it is growing consistently per month (see chapter fourteen), there is hope.

It all boils down to this: you have to figure out how much you think one of those precious hours is worth. I'm often amazed at people who would drive for a half an hour round-trip to save a fiver buying a new pair of jeans but yet they wouldn't work in a job for £10 per hour. That doesn't make any sense whatsoever. If an hour of your time is not worth £10 (or a half hour worth £5), then don't waste time driving around trying to save that amount of money. Realising that my hours are precious and putting a monetary value on my time has given me a different outlook on life.

Having said all that, I do live in the real world and for most people, a regular job is essential. We all have rent or mortgages to pay, school books to buy, food to put on our table and the rest of it. So the idea of trading full-time may be unrealistic right now. If you find yourself in this situation, don't fret. Trade when you can (although not sporadically) and over time, you may earn yourself a nice second income. Who knows, after a number of years, you may be in a position to look at going full-time or even taking a few months off to try it out. Not everyone wants to go full-time though and there are plenty of people who enjoy the security of their job but also enjoy having a side income from another source. It may be simply to pay for a holiday, a meal out, a few pints or even to keep the brain active- everyone has different reasons for trading and everyone's statement will be different. Think long and hard about the reasons you want to spend your hours trading and what you expect to achieve by doing so. If you spend ten hours per week trading and after one year you haven't made any money, ask the hard questions: could I have spent those 520 hours in a better way? If you are doing really well at trading but work in a low-paying job, are you utilising your time the best you can? You don't have to jump in with two feet; a lot of successful traders I know tested the waters first and took a number of years to make the transition from their regular job to full-time trader. Have a good think about your attitude to money and time when coming up with statement number one.

EXAMPLE STATEMENT NUMBER ONE

My aim is to create a second income to supplement my regular wages. Ideally, I'd like to earn between £50 and £70 per week on average based on my current bank size but I will review this figure up or down depending on my progress and how easy or difficult I find trading to be. I realise that some weeks will be bad and some will be good and my goal is simply an average figure. If I'm losing money over time, I will scale down my bank and trade with minimum stakes until such a time that I'm regularly producing a profit. If I'm spending a lot of time trading and not making any money, I promise to ask myself the hard questions and think about whether my time would be best spent on other pursuits. The reason I want a second income is because I want to enjoy life a bit better. The hours I have each week are precious, including the hours I spend trading. I want more money to enjoy myself. I like meals out, I like holidays and I like having extra money to take time off work to spend with my family. Having extra money allows me to take time off for myself. Trading can offer this to me but only if I'm disciplined. In the longer term (around 5 years), I may take a career break from my regular job to experience trading full-time provided I have built up enough capital and my trading is going very well. It's a nice dream to have for the future although I'm taking this one step at a time and I'll cross that bridge when I come to it. For now, I'll concentrate on being the best trader that I can during the limited hours available to me.

2. How much time can I devote to trading?

This will vary greatly as everyone's situation is different. Those with a traditional 9-5 full-time job may only be able to trade in the evenings and at weekends. Others may have hours which allow them to trade during the day. Obviously, you also need to allow for time off for yourself and your family. For a while, I was working a five-day week and then trading on both my days off (and some evenings too when the summer racing was on). This was bad for my mental and physical health and working/trading seven days per week had me burned out. Plan your time carefully and allow for some time off away from the game. No matter what your working situation, my advice is to get yourself a good sports calendar (there are loads available online) and take half an hour every Monday morning to take a look at the week ahead. What are the major events? Will there be enough liquidity in the markets to make it worthwhile? Obviously, Saturday is one of the biggest days of the week for sports so if you are free that day, pencil it in. But if you are free some other day, you have to ask yourself whether it is likely you will make money. If not, take some time out and take the missus to the pictures or whatever. I've wasted many hours trading below average evening racing meetings throughout the years, making very little money while doing so. As mentioned earlier, time is precious so don't waste it in front of a computer if you don't have to. Today, I pick and choose my events carefully. Also, consider whether your personality is suited to one long trading session (such as all day Saturday) or whether you perform best in short bursts (such as an hour a day). Some people take time to get into the swing of things and get a feel for the markets so trading for a full day once a week may suit their personality. But others prefer the short-burst approach as you carry less baggage from earlier trades. If you are trading full-time, you should still have a look at a sports calendar and pick out the days which are likely to provide the best opportunities. Personally, I love to see a day with a number of horse race meetings — with races scheduled to take place around every ten minutes. I'd much sooner trade on a day like that rather than a day with one meeting with a race every half hour. But very busy days can also prove troublesome as races overlap etc. You have to take a look at the calendar and make a decision. If you are trading on a day where events are overlapping, do you need to pick a few events and stick with them? As I say, it's no different to any other job and you need to schedule time off too. If I decide to take a Sunday off, for example, I don't change my mind following a woeful Saturday. I stick to the trading times I allotted for myself on the Monday morning. You must also allow time for research. Research comes in many forms and includes reading books about trading, attending trading courses, reading about your chosen sport, analysing your records and past trades, updating your trading plan and statements etc. For me, the best time to do this is early in the morning before the sporting day has begun. If there is racing or football on while I'm trying to do some research, I get distracted easily. I also set aside some time for my health. That means pencilling in some time each week to go jogging and allowing time to buy and cook some healthy food. I've met many traders who end up overweight and unhealthy as they are slumped in front of a computer all day and don't eat proper meals as they feel they will miss something by taking an hour out to go running or cook a decent meal. This is why it's important to schedule your hours for both trading and other activities before the week begins. Once you start trading, it's all too easy to get swept away by it all. When you begin a trading session, it's actually hard to stop because when you are losing, you feel like trading your way out and when you are winning, you don't want to stop earning money. To counteract this, set up a timetable and stick to it rigidly.

EXAMPLE STATEMENT NUMBER TWO

I can devote roughly 12-16 hours per week to trading. I will trade each Saturday as it is one of the busiest days for sport and I will also trade for an hour or two each evening. I will re-visit this statement when the summer evening racing begins and ends and I will also return to this statement anytime there is a major sporting event such as the World Cup or European Championships. I will clear my schedule to trade during the big racing events such as Cheltenham and Royal Ascot. My trading time will be allocated each Monday morning but while doing this, I will also allocate time for spending with my family, keeping fit and eating healthily. I won't allow a good or bad day of trading to make me deviate from my timetable. When having a day off from trading, I won't bug the hell out of my friends and family by logging into my phone and checking prices on Betfair. On a day off, I won't jump on the computer for a few minutes just to have a look — this often leads to reckless trading. A day off will mean just that.

3. What strategies will I use?

This list of strategies to use should be short until you become quite experienced and master a few. Again, this all comes down to your style. Do you prefer scalping or swing trading? Most people's personality will suit one kind or the other. Adapt a style to suit your personality, although don't be a slave to that. When I first began trading, I always went for scalping as I liked the regular little victories it gave. I couldn't bear to wait around for swing trades to go my way, cutting my losses each time it didn't. But over time, I began to try new things (always with small stakes) and now I'm not so reliant on scalping anymore. What I'm saying is this: you will most likely have a preference for either swing or scalp trading but make sure you try out both for a reasonable amount of time before making a decision on what type of trader you are. Don't assume you know. Once you have decided to focus, write down what particular strategies you are going to use. At the beginning, it's best to keep these strategies to a minimum. Try to master one before moving on to the next. But remember, not all strategies will work for you. If you've tried something for a few weeks and you can't seem to make money, don't feel bad about scrapping it. But avoid jumping from one strategy to another trying to find the Holy Grail — it doesn't exist in trading. Make yourself an expert in one or two areas before moving on and trying new things.

EXAMPLE STATEMENT NUMBER THREE

I enjoy resistance point trading as the concepts are simple. For the next two months, I will only trade resistance points in order to understand how the markets react around these prices. I will not attempt to trade other strategies during this time. If I'm not successful, I will reduce my stakes to an absolute minimum or even consider dropping this strategy completely. I will keep a notebook by my side to record my thoughts and I will record which type of markets the strategy performs best in, all the time being conscious that winning and losing streaks are expected in any trading strategy. I won't over-react to either a winning or losing streak. If I'm successful, I will gradually increase my stakes, keeping in mind that the dynamics and outcomes can be different once the stakes get larger. When I'm very comfortable with resistance point trading, I will add another strategy to my portfolio but I will use the new strategy in separate markets to ensure I don't get muddled. I will only try out a new strategy when I'm happy I've mastered the one before it, or else when I've dropped the one before it due to a lack of success.

4. What is a comfortable level of risk for me?

The answers here will relate to question number one and two as the amount of time and money you can spend on trading will mostly define your risk. When we talk about risk, we need to look at it from two angles. Firstly, what is the overall amount of money you can afford to lose on this project? Is it £500? £1,000? £5,000? £10,000? How are you going to finance this project? Is it from savings? A bank loan? A credit card? If it's from a credit card or bank loan, you have to consider the interest you will be paying on that loan. If your credit card is charging you 17% APR and you are making 10% per year by trading, it's not really a viable business is it? My advice would be to save up an amount and then lodge it, rather than getting a loan. This is especially true if you are a beginner as it could be a couple of years before you show a profit (if at all). How much you can spend and where you get the money from will depend on your circumstances but don't ignore the interest you will be paying if you get a loan to fund your trading business. Interest on a loan is a cost to your trading business. You can pretend it's not there and try to convince yourself you are making a profit but if the profit you make is negated by a loan repayment with interest then you are only fooling yourself. I know a couple of guys who just about turn a small profit on their trading and they are rightly proud to do so. However, a number used credit cards to initially fund their bank and now have maxed out balances at high interest rates. Just imagine, these guys have the skill and brains to turn a profit in this difficult game yet they can't recognise some simple maths; the credit card bill is gobbling up all the profit from their hard work.

Also, if you have a large sum of money to invest, remember that you don't need to lodge all of it into your trading account. You won't be using it for the most part. I like to have only a quarter of my total trading budget actually lodged in my account. So, for example, if you had twenty grand set aside, you should be happy to keep five grand in your trading account and keep the fifteen in a bank account which earns interest but also allows easy access. Remember, if you are trading with your full capital, you may be exposing yourself to risk and there's also the temptation to chase losses. You need a slush fund kept aside for when things are not going so well and you can top up your trading account as necessary. Likewise, when things are going very well and you are earning some nice money, cream some of it off and put it into your savings. There's really no point in leaving money idle in betting accounts; it only earns interest for the betting company and not you.

Once you've decided how much you can allocate overall, you then need to look at how much you are willing to risk per trade and also what your risk/reward ratio will be per trade. Again, this will come down to personality and also whether you are a swing trader or a scalper but I'd recommend that you never risk more than a certain percentage of your overall bank per trade. If you decide that you are willing to risk no more than 2% per trade, you must work out your stakes that way, based on price.

Risk/reward is the amount you hope to gain from a winning trade. If you are scalping, you might want to risk a tick for every tick you earn so your risk/reward would be 1:1 (in other words, you are looking for even money winners). If you were swing trading, your risk/reward ratio would be much higher. You could decide on a 6:1 ratio for swing trades which means you would be looking to earn six times the amount on a good trade that you are willing to lose on a bad trade (so you are looking for 6/1 winners).

EXAMPLE STATEMENT NUMBER FOUR

I am willing to risk £5,000 in total on my trading business. I will keep £4,000 of this in a bank account as a back-up and trade with the remaining £1,000 left in the account. I will fund this trading business through savings as I realise that paying interest on any loan will have an impact on my overall profit, since the margins are already extremely tight. On the strategy I use, the expected risk/reward ratio is between 1:1 and 1:3. Being aware of my risk/reward ratio will allow me to see if my strike rate is as it should be.

5. What kind of records am I going to keep?

First of all, if you are not reasonably proficient in Excel, you should head down to your local library and borrow a book to get yourself up to speed. You need to be able to sort, filter, create charts, run staking plans etc. if you want to get the best from your record keeping. Nothing too difficult mind you, just the basic functions of a spreadsheet. If you don't want to pay for Excel, there's free open source software similar to *Microsoft Office* out there you can use such as Open Office. There's no point in keeping good records if you've no way of analysing them. I knew nothing about Excel until a friend in college suggested I was wasting a lot of time writing all my bets (and everything about them) down by hand in a ledger and doing the sums manually. Initially, I was sceptical and didn't want to spend the time learning but now I find Excel an absolutely essential skill to have as a trader. All that said, there has to be a reason why you record certain pieces of information. If you are trading horseracing, for example, there's no point in recording what colour the jockey silks were. Only record practical information that you are likely to use when reviewing your results. Things like the stakes used, field size, type of market (I write down on a scale of ten how stable/volatile I found the market), type of race, amount of money matched, price of the favourite, type of trade etc. are all likely to be useful when checking out your results to see which type of races suit your trading style. You should also set time aside (preferably when the markets are closed) to review your records, perhaps as regularly as once a week.

EXAMPLE STATEMENT NUMBER FIVE

I will record as much about each trade as practical. I will keep a notebook beside the computer to record this information and then transfer it to an Excel spreadsheet when I'm done trading for the day. On a certain day per week, I will get up two hours earlier than normal to review my records to see which areas I am performing well in and which areas need work. All the time, I will remain aware that small data samples can be misleading so I won't make any rash decisions based on the data until it has built up substantially. If I find that I am performing particularly strongly over a long period of time in a certain type of trade, I will consider specialising in that type of trade.

6. What are my rules for when I have a winning/losing day?

Trading is an ongoing process where a single winning or losing day shouldn't matter too much in the longer term and as such, it doesn't seem sensible to introduce rules for particular days be they good or bad. We shouldn't get too excited about a good day or get too down about a bad day and until recently, I've avoided making rules for good or bad days. All that said, we are not robots either and it's almost impossible not to compartmentalise our trading time into days, weeks and months. The truth is, our mood is affected when we are making loads of money or suffering heavy losses and it's when we are in these emotional states that we make mistakes, chase our losses, or trade with cockiness. If you are having a fantastic day of trading, you may not want to stop but sometimes it makes sense to take some time off and bank some money. A couple of years ago, I was having a cracking day and had made in the region of €400 in the space of a couple of hours. I considered stopping but since I was on a roll, I decided to continue and trade the evening races. Unfortunately, I started losing on the evening races; nothing big at first but enough to chip away at my earlier hard work. I should have quit when my total for the day dropped to around €300 but the problem was psychological. The €400 figure had been anchored in my brain and I felt an overwhelming urge to get back to that level. Even though a €300 profit is fantastic by most standards, it suddenly wasn't good enough and the €400 mark represented a successful day for me. Stupidly, I made some reckless trades and when the total profit was down to about €50, I finally gave in and closed the laptop lid. A losing day can have an effect on our confidence and may push us into decisions we may not have made otherwise as we attempt to claw our way back. We've all heard the phrase 'quit while you're ahead' but in trading, you need to learn to quit while you are behind too. I now have rules for dealing with winning and losing days whereby I'll quit if I win/lose a certain amount. As I've said numerous times, daily results shouldn't matter too much in the overall scheme of things but stepping away from the computer in certain circumstances can help to stop us trading on emotion. If you abhor the idea of quitting when you lose or win a certain amount, at least consider reducing your stakes considerably to avoid the large losses that so often come when we trade on emotion.

EXAMPLE STATEMENT NUMBER SIX
While I realise that trading is a long-term business where daily results shouldn't matter too much, I'm also aware that losing or winning a large sum of money in a short space of time can have an effect on my emotions. Trading when emotional is usually bad practice so if I lose €200 in a particular trading session, I will quit for the day as it means I'm just not 'in the zone' for whatever reason. If I make more than €400 in a trading session, I will consider rewarding myself with the rest of the day off or at the very least, reduce my stakes. This will stop me be becoming over-confident or chasing losses should the figure drop back down.

7. What are my rules about withdrawing money?
It should come as no surprise that a good deal of people with betting accounts have never clicked the 'withdraw' button. Sadly, they've clicked the 'deposit' button many times over. Of course your objective when starting out should be to protect your capital so it could be some time before you are in a position to withdraw money — but when you do get there, you should have some sort of plan, rather than taking a haphazard approach. One of the main problems with keeping money in a betting account is that it doesn't feel real — and that's especially true if we have won it. Money we have won (or earned though trading) is often treated differently than the

rest of our money even though this makes no sense whatsoever. Do you have this attitude? Do you like to 'play up' your winnings in an attempt to maximise it? If the answer is 'yes', you need to re-evaluate your relationship with money and ask yourself why you treat money from other sources (your wages for example) differently than money you got from trading or betting. After all, it's all just pieces of paper, metaphorically speaking of course. I've seen traders work for months building up banks and then blow it all during a moment of madness. I've done it myself. Would these moments of madness have happened had I withdrawn some winnings occasionally and not got too cocky? Probably not. When it comes to withdrawing money these days, I like to take an approach that allows me to enjoy the fruits of my labour while allowing my bank to grow. The important thing is to make sure you are rewarding yourself when some sort of criteria is met. What's the point otherwise? I often re-invest the money I withdraw in other things like trading education and books but I also make sure I keep a bit aside and treat myself to the odd expensive bottle of wine or perhaps take the missus out for a meal etc. It's all about work-life balance and it's no different to any other job in that respect.

EXAMPLE STATEMENT NUMBER SEVEN

Building and protecting my bank is important to me but so too is enjoying the monetary rewards that trading can bring. That's why I do it. If I double my bank, I will withdraw 20% of it. So when my £5,000 starting bank becomes £10,000, I will withdraw £2,000. This still leaves me with a decent-sized trading bank of £8,000 and also allows me to enjoy the fruits of my labour. Out of the £2,000, I will spend around £500 on trading education such as books, courses and software, I will save £1,000 for the 'rainy day' and I will spend £500 on my family, charity and some nice evenings out or a weekend away. This statement will be reviewed once my bank has doubled and the money withdrawn. I will then come up with a new plan for future withdrawals, based on the 20% model.

8. What are the associated costs of trading and how am I going to fund them?

Apart from the obvious cost of setting up a trading bank, you will need to consider the extra costs associated with trading and think about how they will be funded. As mentioned earlier, I think it's best to fund your trading from savings rather than a loan as any interest paid on a loan is an extra expense that could negate your profit. Eventually, it is hoped that your trading profits should fund your expenses. What sort of costs are we looking at? Well, a decent computer with plenty of memory and speed is a must. I've heard of applications which allow you to trade on iPads and tablets but I reckon it's going to be a couple of years before people are comfortable trading fully on mobile devices. I'm certainly no Luddite and I use my tablet and my iPhone all the time to place bets and get in or out of longer term trades. Personally, I look forward to the day when I can trade wherever I want from a tablet or some kind of mobile device but for the moment, the speeds and functionality are a long way off the traditional computer. Alongside a computer, you will need, of course, a high-speed Internet connection. Every region and country differs but it's best to get the fastest speed available, even if that does cost you an extra few quid per month. The difference between a very high-speed line and a regular congested line may only be the price of a couple of losing trades per month — but a faster line can cut out some losing trades or certainly give you a slight edge in a fast-moving market so it should be worth it. It may not be practical to have a back-up computer and connection when you are starting out but when you start to trade in large sums and are leaving yourself exposed to thousands of pounds on a given market, you need to know you can get out of a trade should your computer or Internet connection crash. If the electricity goes down, can you get a mobile connection on a battery powered tablet for example? Can you access the market quickly? When you are trading with serious amounts, you may need two computers, two Internet service providers and be sure everything is charged. Aside from computers, you will need to read as much as you can to get new ideas. As yet, there are very few books out there on betting exchange trading (hence this one!) but I'd encourage readers to get stuck into some financial trading books. The concepts are largely the same and who knows you may, like me, add a new string to your bow and become a S&P 500, FOREX or FTSE trader alongside your sports activity. Trading camps and courses can be expensive but some are worth the money. I've been on a number of training courses (both sports trading and financial trading) and while some were a good investment, others were just one long sales pitch for a book, system or some type of software. A good web search on the course before you attend is a must to avoid the charlatans. When it comes to screens for your computer, only buy what you need. A multi-screen trading setup looks mighty impressive but if you are only using one screen at a time, then it's pointless. Any good businessman will tell you that penny pinching is the name of the game so only buy a new 'toy' such as an extra monitor if you really need it. Finally, there are your subscription costs for your trading software and also your subscription to your sports channels on TV. Like any business, these must be factored in. Remember, you are not truly making money in the business of trading until you can easily cover these costs through your trading activity.

EXAMPLE STATEMENT NUMBER EIGHT
Like any business, trading has a number of setup and also ongoing costs. I will endeavour to keep these costs to a minimum although I do realise that some expenses such as books or trading courses are an investment rather than a dead cost. I will only consider myself a successful trader when I'm making enough to cover all costs and also make a profit. This will take time. Some businesses can take a number of years before they become profitable and I don't expect to do it overnight. When I am consistently making good money, I will endeavour to re-invest a percentage of it back into my business in the form of equipment, education or software etc. but I will avoid buying unnecessary 'toys' for myself as these chip away at my profits.

9. Other than money, how am I going to reward myself for all my hard work?

This is another question which ties in with some earlier statements. Obviously, the main driver for trading is financial gain and successful traders are paid for their efforts by their profits. But I believe that you need to reward yourself from time to time with something other than money. Cheltenham, for example, is the busiest time of the year for those involved in racing and win lose or draw, I'll take a few days off afterwards to treat myself after a hectic week. If you've had a cracking week of trading, why not consider taking an extra day off? Sometimes we can get so caught up in our trading that we forget to look after ourselves and also forget to enjoy ourselves. I've seen people spend every minute they have in front of the screen, much to the detriment of their family life. When you are making good money, be sure to enjoy the financial rewards but don't forget too that time off should be a reward in itself. It may be simply taking an afternoon off to spend with the family, a DVD with the other half or going to a sporting event. While you must work extremely hard in this game, you don't have to trade every possible minute of the day and win or lose, hard work must be rewarded (as long as costs are kept to a minimum).

EXAMPLE STATEMENT NUMBER NINE
While I hope to make good profits from trading, not every day, week or month is going to be profitable, no matter how hard I work. But it is still important to reward myself when I've worked very hard even if I have lost money during the period. This helps avoid burnout and also allows me to enjoy other activities outside of trading. After a particularly busy time (like Royal Ascot or Cheltenham), I will take three days off trading to relax and recharge the batteries, regardless of whether I've made money or not. I will make note of the amount of time I spend trading for each session, add them up, and when I reach 100 hours, I will arrange to take a half-day to spend time with my family. For every 150 hours spent trading, I will reward myself with a nice bottle of wine or perhaps attend a sporting event. These rewards are a payment for all my hard work so I will endeavour to take them regardless of my trading results.

10. How much money or time am I willing to spend on blogging, networking and education?
I've mentioned education a number of times earlier with regard to books and courses etc. but there's also a wealth of information to be gleaned

online through networking, forums, chatrooms, blogs and social networking sites. Trading can be a solitary business so it's worth signing up to one or two forums which allow interaction with fellow traders. Often, you can get your questions answered and may come across some profitable ideas. Most of the major trading software retailers have forums which you can join to discuss your trading. It's true to say that there are idiots, boasters and bullshitters all over the internet but in my experience, most other traders on forums and other groups are usually helpful. Realise that you don't know everything, that there are better traders out there than you, and that you can never stop learning. So if you have a question, go online and post it up — it's highly likely that someone has been in your situation before. Likewise, I will often answer questions from traders who are starting out as I realise just how daunting the whole experience can be. Blogs can also be very useful. A blog can be used as a diary to report your progress to the outside world. Many bloggers will set themselves a challenge (how long will it take to double my bank for example) and post their thoughts and results each day. I've done this myself and it is great for discipline, building contacts, promoting yourself or your ideas and avoiding loneliness. Don't be disheartened if your blog is only getting a couple of hits per day. Over time, it will take off, especially if you are honest about your experiences and your results. Put up links to other blogs you enjoy reading and they may reciprocate, thus enhancing your readership. There have been times I've blogged away with no responses for weeks and I wondered if I was wasting my time. But then out of the blue, I might get a writing job offer from some newspaper or website which has stumbled across my blog and are looking for an article on trading. Keeping the blog up-to-date is essential and it's also important to respond quickly to any questions or comments you may receive.

EXAMPLE STATEMENT NUMBER TEN
I will set aside time and money for books, courses and seminars to help my trading education. Trading can be a lonely business and I realise the importance of keeping in touch with other people. I will spend time reading the online trading forums and groups, and join the one which appeals the

most. I will try to get to know, and keep in touch with other traders. I will set up a themed blog (eg: My £1,000 challenge) and update daily once the trading day is done.

SOME FINAL THOUGHTS

WELL if you've got this far, let me thank you for reading my book and I sincerely hope it has served its purpose of giving you a better understanding of how the markets work. In this world, there are not many pursuits which can be so rewarding yet so demanding at the same time. Of course, there can never be one definitive book on trading with a set of rules that makes easy cash for everyone, and the market is always adjusting itself to close any anomalies or loopholes. The truth is, no-one knows what will work ten years from now and that's part of the challenge. But if I've given you some background information which may help you earn money and encouraged you to come up with your own ideas too, then my book has done its job. For me, the fun in trading is about trying out new things, pitting my wits against the best of the best and hopefully, coming out on top over time. Sitting on my laurels is not an option. The challenge of making a profit through trading is daunting but far from impossible and like everything, practice is the real key. There are no short-cuts. While this happens to be my first book, I'm hoping it's not my last. Indeed, the world of trading and betting is an ever-changing landscape and there's a surprise around every corner so I'm sure there will be plenty to write about in the future. In the meantime, feel free to keep an eye on my website or blog, and if you have any comments, criticism, questions or suggestions please send an email to waynebaileyracing@gmail.com .

To finish off, I was going to wish you, the reader 'good luck' but luck is not something we can sit and wait for. So instead, let me sign off by simply saying 'work hard'.

Wayne Bailey, January 2014

WAYNE BAILEY RACING

Highly successful place lays system based on WBR's unique
jockey ratings. Over £5,000 in profit to a £10 stake.*
Past results:

Year	No. bets	Successful lays	Strike rate	Profit to £10
2015	1902	1082	56.89	£165.17
2014	3466	1984	57.24	£1,782.10
2013	2403	1355	56.39	£1,802.60
2012	3871	2139	55.26	£108.00
2011	3759	2075	55.2	£251.50
2010	4220	2333	55.28	-£67.30
2009	3245	1718	52.94	£566.90
2008	2200	1202	54.64	£659.60
Total	25066	13888	55.48	£5,268.57

* Results last updated June 2015

For more information, visit www.waynebaileyracing.com

PROOFED TO RACING-INDEX

* All bets recorded to a £10 fixed stake at Betfair place SP. Results
assume the layer is paying the maximum 5% commission.

RECOMMENDED READING

Ariely, Dan. *Predictably Irrational: The Hidden Forces that Shape Our Decisions.* Harper Collins, 2009. ISBN: 978-0007256532.

Aronson, Elliot & Tavris, Carol. *Mistakes Were Made (but Not by Me): Why We Justify Foolish Beliefs, Bad Decisions and Hurtful Acts.* Pinter & Martin Ltd, 2013. ISBN: 978-1780660356.

Carter, John F. *Mastering the Trade: Proven Techniques for Profiting from Intraday and Swing Trading Setups.* McGraw-Hill Professional, 2006. ISBN: 978-0071459587.

Douglas, Mark. *The Disciplined Trader: Developing Winning Attitudes.* Prentice Hall, 2000. ISBN: 978-0132157575.

Elder, Alexander. *Come into My Trading Room.* John Wiley & Sons, 2002. ISBN: 978-0471225348.

Farleigh, Richard. *Taming the Lion: 100 Secret Strategies for Investing.* Harriman House Publishing, 2005. ISBN: 978-1897597620.

Kahneman, Daniel. *Thinking, Fast and Slow.* Penguin, 2012. ISBN: 978-0141033570.

Taleb, Nassim Nicholas. *Fooled by Randomness: The Hidden Role of Chance in Life and in the Markets.* Penguin, 2007. ISBN: 978-0141031484.